TAMIL CLASSICS

SELLATHAMBY SRISKANDARAJAH

authorHOUSE®

AuthorHouse™ UK Ltd.
500 Avebury Boulevard
Central Milton Keynes, MK9 2BE
www.authorhouse.co.uk
Phone: 08001974150

First published by AuthorHouse 11/9/2011

ISBN: 978-1-4389-4196-7 (sc)
ISBN: 978-1-4389-4197-4 (hc)
ISBN: 978-1-4670-0362-9 (e)

To

my late father in law and Tamil Scholar

Dr Vidwan K.N. Velan

Contents

ACKNOWLEDGEMENTS

Although this small work is intended for Tamil readers, nevertheless with a view to obtaining a nonpartisan opinion on it from a native English speaker, I showed the draft of this book to Mr. Alastair Robin McGlashan, a scholar in Greek classics and Tamil studies. Mr. McGlashan, who is a many-faceted scholar, has just completed the translation of Cekkiḻār's Periya Purāṇam which contains more than four thousand verses. I am indebted to Mr. McGlashan for the nice Foreword he has written and for the many constructive suggestions he offered during the preparation of this book. I thank him wholeheartedly.

Professor V. C. Kulandaiswamy, a poet of great repute and one time Vice Chancellor of the Indira Gandhi National Open University, has added weight and value to my book by his valuable and constructive Introduction. I am grateful to him for the honour he has done me.

Dr. Avvai Natarajan, a Tamil scholar of international reputation and emeritus Vice Chancellor of the Tamil University of Tanjore was kind enough to look through the book at the manuscript stage and to write a wonderful Appreciation. I am eternally indebted to him.

I will be failing in my duty if I fail to record the help rendered by Miss Thulasi Mageswaran M.Sc, Mr.K.Jeyakumar FIAB, MAAT and Mrs.Shobana Janakan M.Sc all of whom had the indefatigable patience to type out the various drafts of this book which I amended and modified times without number. I thank them all wholeheartedly. I am grateful to Mr Arunan Sriskandarajah LL.M for the beautiful cover design of this book as well as for the many other useful suggestions of artistic significance.

Finally I thank Author House Publishers for publishing my work beautifully.

S. Sriskandarajah
66, Westrow Gardens
Seven Kings, Ilford,
Essex IG3 9NF
United Kingdom

PREFACE

The Tamils are the proud owners of a rich treasury of literature. Though they are an ancient race, still they don't have a country of their own. In India, they occupy a state called Tamil Nadu, which has no sovereign status. The political storm in Sri Lanka has forced the Eelam Tamils to flee Sri Lanka and to seek refuge on foreign soil in the West. The situation in the West is not conducive to the study of Tamil literature and other matters relating to Tamil art and culture. Their situation is such that willy-nilly Tamil children are compelled to pay less and less attention to the study of Tamil language and literature. Such unfortunate children cannot be expected to gain access to Tamil literature through their imperfect knowledge of Tamil language. However, not to make an attempt to teach them the great gems of Tamil literature would be a crime.

I therefore thought of the idea of giving them a foretaste of Tamil literature through English. I made a similar attempt fifteen years ago and produced a book in English called "The Ethical Essence of The Tamils" which is a commentary on selected Tirukkuṟaḷ couplets. The present book is a fruit of my second attempt. If my experience with my earlier book is anything to go by, I can hope that the children of the expatriate Tamil community will find this small work very useful.

I have selected the poems for this book randomly. Though I had wished to give a typical example from each of the collections of the Ancient period, the fear that such a laudable attempt would be expensive and time consuming has prevented me from so doing.

I started work on these literary paintings almost fifteen years ago. Some of the episodes in this book were published in a fortnightly called *Tamil Nation*. When the publication of *Tamil Nation* was discontinued, my urge for writing such literary pieces also sagged though I continued to write them once in a blue moon and preserved the manuscripts.

This book contains thirty-seven of such paintings, the majority of which are scenes from the ancient classics. *Kampaṉ* and *Avvaiyār* are great names although strictly they do not belong to the classical period. Their works are of commendable quality and reputation. In recognition of their merit I have chosen a few verses from their works for the purpose of this book. The late Mr.J.V.Chelliah, a great Tamil scholar of Sri Lanka who translated many ancient Tamil verses into English, declared with pride and justly that we are the trustees of a rich heritage, and it is our duty to share with the rest of the world, the best that has been said and written by our forefathers. I am glad that through this small work I am able to fulfil at least a part of his wish.

This book is primarily intended for expatriate Tamil children. However I am confident that non Tamil speakers who are interested in literature also will find the book useful and interesting.

S.Sriskandarajah, *B.Sc., LL.M*

FOREWORD

I count it an honour to be invited to contribute a few words by way of a Foreword to Mr Sriskandarajah's "Scenes from Tamil Classics". I greatly appreciate the service which the author is performing, by means of this and his other published works, to popularize Tamil literature among those who cannot read it in the original.

This group of Tamils must of course primarily include the children of Tamil families which have come from South Asian countries and settled in the West. More than some other immigrant communities, Tamil people in the United Kingdom seem to tend naturally and easily to become assimilated to the host culture. There are gains in that, but also losses. Particularly, as the children of such families are educated within the English school system, they are in danger of growing up unable fluently to read and write their mother tongue. Thus they lose touch with the riches of the culture in which their parents were reared in India and Sri Lanka.

The children of first generation immigrants are inescapably placed in a situation of great difficulty. They are caught in what must be a most uncomfortable tension between the culture of the school and the ambient society on the one hand, and that of the family on the other. At a deeper level this can only give rise to profound questions about their sense of identity. Who are they, where do they belong, and whose norms do they adopt? I applaud the strenuous efforts made by the author of the present work and many like him who through voluntary weekend classes in many parts of London attempt to nurture in the rising generation knowledge of, and a sense of belonging to, their traditional culture.

Of course, the entirety of the British population has to be included in the number of those who cannot read the Tamil classics in the original. But, sad to say, the level of interest not only in Tamil, but more generally in the languages and culture of the Indian sub-continent as a whole seems currently to be at a very low ebb. In the old days of the Raj there were many British people whose whole working lives were spent in the East. Some of them became proficient in Indian languages and extremely knowledgeable in various fields of Indian studies. But those days are long gone, and British contact with South Asia is limited to fleeting visits by tourists and business people, who may indeed be impressed and fascinated by what they see of the local cultures, but have neither the time nor the inclination to embark on deeper study. There seems to be little prospect of this situation changing in the foreseeable future.

That being said, I have to disclose my own interest in this matter, and acknowledge that I have not completely given up all hope for the English–speaking West. For I have myself recently published a translation of *Cekkiḻār's Periya Purāṇam* into English prose. So perhaps all is not yet lost! That publication is a concrete expression of my own desire that the rich heritage of Tamil culture and religion should more widely be known and valued in the West.

However, Mr Sriskandarajah's work is addressed primarily to the former group, namely the children of Tamil immigrants who are in danger of becoming increasingly alienated from their cultural roots. And what he provides is a series of brief extracts from the classics together with a wide ranging survey of classical

Tamil literature. Each poem or individual stanza from a poem is given with the original Tamil text, an English translation and an expository amplification.

One of the characteristics of early Tamil poetry which immediately strikes the modern reader is its under-stated, allusive quality. For example, in the poems of the Caṅkam age, emotions are not flaunted, or worn on the sleeve. Nor are the situations in which the protagonists find themselves described in exhaustive detail. Rather, much of the context and of the emotional content has to be inferred from oblique references to the various modes of the *akam* and *puṟam* poetic conventions, which the reader is expected to pick up and understand.

This restrained, suggestive quality is also a feature of some early Greek poetry. Here are two examples from the work of Sappho of Lesbos, who lived around 600 BC (my own translations of nos.149 and 156 from the Oxford Book of Greek Verse, ed. G Murray et al, the Clarendon Press, Oxford, 1930):

Mother dear, I can no longer ply the loom;
For I am overwhelmed with longing for a certain boy
This is all the doing of slender Aphrodite.

The moon has set,
So too the Pleiades,
Midnight is past
The hours drag by;
And as for me,
I sleep alone

The parallel will at once be clear, I think. Both the Caṅkam poets and Sappho state just enough to bring the scene alive, and leave the rest to the imagination of the reader.

Although in the ethical literature of the Tamils we are not spectators of an unfolding drama in the same way, a comparably terse, epigrammatic quality is seen in these two or four-line aphorisms. For the most part, the injunctions are given in a highly condensed, generalized form, without application to specific, lived examples. The nearest parallel to this that is likely to be familiar to Western readers is the wisdom literature to be found in the Hebrew bible, in such books as Proverbs and the Wisdom of Solomon.

In his "Scenes from Tamil Classics", Mr Sriskandarajah deals with his selected extracts, which virtually all exhibit the characteristics described above, in a more or less uniform way. That is to say, he paints in the details of the story or the situation which the poet has left unsaid, drawing out the inferences and making explicit the allusions lying dormant in the text. By so doing, he brings the scene alive within a specific, reconstructed context and prevents the eye of the reader passing too swiftly over the text with a superficial reading. He makes the reader think about the action and the feeling expressed, and enables him/her to appreciate the artistry of the poet.

It could be said that in the *Periya Purāṇam*, the author *Cekkiḻār* performs a not entirely dissimilar service for the authors of the *Tēvāram* hymns. For in his lives of *Appar, Campantar* and *Cuntarar,* he frequently notes in his narrative the precise circumstances in which particular hymns were composed, for example, after *Appar's* deliverance from his stomach pain and his conversion to Saivism, when the Pallava king sends his minions to arrest him, *Cekkiḻār* records that *Appar* sang the hymn beginning with the words "We are no one's subjects" (*Periya Purāṇam 1358, cf. Tēvāram vi.98*). Set in this very specific context, the hymn takes on added depth of meaning, as a courageous defiance of the king, in a situation of very real danger. The true devotee fears no threat or punishment, whether in this life or the next, and lives his life in freedom from the demands of all earthly authorities, trusting in the provision and protection of his Lord.

To bring alive the contemporary relevance of one particular group of poems, Mr Sriskandarajah draws upon the experience of the Tamil people in the on-going civil war in Sri Lanka. He finds parallels between that experience and the experience of the poets and their contemporaries nearly two thousand years ago, as described in the *Puṟam* poetry of the Caṅkam age. This makes a striking impact on the reader, and allows the outsider to begin to appreciate the depth of feeling aroused in the Tamil people in the course of their protracted, bloody struggle for justice in Sri Lanka.

It is clear that Mr Sriskandarajah is both widely read and well schooled in the Tamil classics with which he deals. Beyond that, on every page he evinces a deep love of his subject, which is readily communicated to his readers, and thus serves to arouse their interest and enthusiasm also. He leads the reader into a world which is many centuries and thousands of miles distant from our own. But at the same time, he makes it unmistakably plain that the men and women of whom the ancient poets wrote were human beings like ourselves, with interests, feelings and reactions similar to our own.

It is a pleasure to commend this work to a new generation of readers, and indeed to their parents and grandparents also, because there is much for anyone to learn and profit from in these pages. I trust that the torch which the author has lit will kindle a love for Tamil literature in many hearts, and so enrol a company of new enthusiasts to carry that torch forward into the future.

Alastair Robin McGlashan

M.A (Oxford), M.A (Cambridge)

INTRODUCTION

Tamil and Chinese are perhaps the two ancient languages that have endured over three millennia with an unbroken continuity, as literary and spoken languages, renewing and developing and meeting substantially one or more of the social, economic and political needs of the people who use them as their mother tongue.

There are certain characteristics of Tamil that deserve special mention. Tamil is:

1. An ancient language with a literary tradition of over 2500 years;
2. A language associated with one of the greatest civilizations of humanity; and
3. Acknowledged as one of the classical languages of the world comparable to Greek, Latin and Sanskrit.

Tamil is a South Asian language with a global diaspora, covering over sixty countries, accounting for a population of nearly 75 million and enjoying the 17th rank in the world in terms of numbers.

Today the enlightened members of the modern world are jealously guarding two sources of its richness, namely;

1. biodiversity ; and
2. ethnic diversity.

Both are threatened and endangered by the advancement and application of technology that continuously promotes physical changes and globalization.

Panambaranar, in his preface to the great grammatical treatise called Tolkappiam defined the boundaries of Tamil Nadu as follows:

"Tamil world is lying between
The Venkata hills in the North and
Cape Comorin in the South."

These boundaries have now shrunk both in the North and in the South. However, Tamils live today in more than 60 countries, in different numbers, all over the world.

The poet Kulothungan describes the present status as follows:

"The Tamil community
Which once proclaimed
That the world is the common nest
For all humans
Is today a global family"

The Tamils as a race live in many countries; follow different religions; and belong to different parties. In the countries to which their ancestors migrated some 150-200 years ago during the British rule, they maintain their identity only by certain social customs and religious practices such as walking over fire and carrying fire pots on their palms, which are somewhat primitive in nature and may not last long.

The only armour for the Tamils to guard their individuality and identity in future is their mother tongue. Therefore they have to preserve their association with their language (literature), culture and heritage for which knowledge of Tamil is a pre-requisite. The encouraging factor, fortunately, is that there is among the Tamil diaspora an awareness of this need and the Tamil communities in different countries of the world are organising facilities for learning Tamil, practising music and dance and also for celebrating festivals that are peculiar to the Tamils.

Against the background stated in the foregoing paragraphs, the attempt on the part of Mr.Sellathamby Sriskandarajah to introduce the literary heritage of the Tamils to the world of letters in general and to the Tamil diaspora in particular is really a laudable effort. Considering the objective of this book, it is comprehensive in content and the presentation is lucid while the language is elegant.

The author has given a brief history of the Tamil language, the Sri Lankan Tamils and Tamil literature. This serves to provide an overview of the past for the guidance of the readers.

In the chapter on a brief history of Tamil literature, the author has succeeded in emphasizing the uniqueness of Sankam literature while stressing the fact that what is now known as Indian civilization and culture has the contribution of the Tamils as an inseparable component. The literary and philosophical heritage of India is the result of the confluence of two mighty rivers, namely, Sanskrit and Tamil.

The Sankam period of Tamil literature has certain astonishing factors that may not have a parallel in human history. Scholars differ in defining the Sankam age. However it will be safe to state that it covers at least a period of four hundred years beginning from 200BC to 200AD. During this four hundred year period of history, there were 473 poets, more than thirty of whom were women. Again they belonged to almost every profession – there were kings, ministers, carpenters, businessmen, agriculturists, potters, astronomers, doctors and others. In the distant past, literary activity had been the prerogative of the leisured class in every civilization. The universal participation in creative activity in the Sankam period is a phenomenon that requires a deeper study. Mr. Sriskandarajah has shown admirable insight in perceiving this attainment in the history of the Tamils.

The author has succeeded in introducing the classical works of Tamil by covering scenes from the Sankam corpus, post Sankam literature, and also poems from the Bhakti movement.

Ancient Tamil literature bears testimony to the heights attained by Indian literary tradition. It has touched a level of excellence which is a matter of pride, not only for the Tamils, but also for the Indian sub-continent as a whole. Mr. Sriskandarajah, I am glad to record, has in his choice of poems, in the explanation preceding each poem, and in the translation, maintained admirably the poetic element, and succeeded in bringing out the secular character, humanism, serenity, restraint, clarity and universality of the Sankam poems.

To illustrate the mastery of the author in grasping fully the soul of the poem and conveying it with an undiminished appeal, one or two examples will not be out of place here.

Pari, the chieftain of a hill country called Parampu was one among the seven celebrated patrons in Tamil history. The three great rulers of the Pantiya, the Cera and the Cola kingdoms, who could not successfully battle against Pari individually and defeat him, joined together, defeated him, killed him and occupied his territory. Pari had two unmarried daughters who were orphaned and a poem composed by them in their hour of sorrow runs as follows in Mr.Sriskandarajah's translation:

Last month this moon shone bright and clear;
then our father was alive
and our hills were not in the hands of foreigners.
This month the same moon shines;
but the plundering kings have seized our hills
and made us orphans.

(Puranaanooru – 122)

The melancholic scene with two young royal sisters, orphaned rather suddenly, bereft of their property, steeped in grief with emptiness all around finds full expression and touches the hearts of the readers to their very depths. It wrenches our heart with grief.

Another instance of an immortal poem quoted by the author is from Kurunthokai. It describes the union of the young hearts of two lovers who were total strangers before they met and became as indistinguishably united as the rain water that falls on the red soil. The short poem has been rendered in English by Mr. Sriskandarajah as follows:

What has your mother to do with mine?
or what relation is my father to yours?

So how did you and I get to know each other?

But just as the rain water

takes on the colour of the soil on which it falls,so

when we fell in love

our hearts became inseparable.

(Kurunthokai 40)

The rain clouds are far above the ground. The field with red soil lies somewhere on the earth. There is no relationship between the clouds and the soil. They are so far apart. The simile of the rainwater descending from the clouds, mixing indistinguishably with the soil on which if falls, to the two strangers meeting each other, becoming lovers by mutual attraction and getting united is extremely appropriate and memorable. Here is a poem describing the love between the two, whose mothers are strangers, whose fathers are not known to each other. The poem itself does not contain the name of anyone nor of any place or any family. The names of parents, even the names of the lovers are not given. This event can well be ascribed to any couple, in any part of the world, in any period of human history. It is timeless. The Sankam classical poetry is remarkable for universality, serenity, humanism and appeal.

Sanskrit and Tamil were contemporary languages and both have a treasury of ancient literature. The literary treasures of Sanskrit were widely known in advanced countries, at least a full century earlier than Tamil literary works were known.

A Mogul prince, *Tharashuko* by name was fascinated by the Upanishads and he organised the translation of fifty of them into Persian. European scholars translated the *Upanishads* into Latin, making use of the Persian version, at the beginning of the 19th century (1801). Since the close of the 17th century, systematic efforts have been made in India and Europe to translate important Sanskrit works into English and other European languages. As a result they came to be widely known in the West. It was only a century or more later that the Tamil classics were translated, because they all lay in palm-leaf bundles, mostly in the possession of private individuals. They were identified and printed only during the second half of the 19th century. It was when they were made available in print that some efforts were made to have them translated into English and other European languages.

Even today sufficient translations of Tamil works with commentaries are not available. Against this background, Mr. Sriskandarajah's contribution by way of selections from Tamil literary works is a commendable effort to meet a long-felt need.

Walt Whitman, the revolutionary American poet says in his poem entitled 'Shut Not Your Doors':

"Shut not your doors to me proud libraries
For that which was lacking on
All your well filled shelves
Yet needed most I bring".

Mr. Sriskandarajah has brought Tamil classics to the shelves of libraries in European countries. The Tamil diaspora will be eternally grateful to him for an enduring contribution.

Professor V.C Kulandaiswamy

(Former Vice Chancellor – Indira Gandhi National Open University)

APPRECIATION

Ninety years ago, in a grand and morbid gesture, Edmond Larforest, a writer in Haiti, tied a French Larousse dictionary around his neck and jumped off the pier to a watery death. He dramatized, fatally, the artistic drowning of Haitian language and culture in a powerful and hegemonic tradition. It may look an extreme step for the sake of the language. However it shows his love and passion for his mother tongue. In the same way the Tamils' love and passion for their classic Tamil have seen similar expressions.

Language is an integral part of human existence, vital to a sense of identity and therefore to emotional health. There is a natural connection between the language spoken by a social group and that group's self image. From this citizenship or membership, the group draws a distinct strength and pride, a social importance, and a feeling of belonging in a historical space. The closer you move to your mother tongue, the deeper you move into the safety zone of a sense of self.

My good friend and learned luminary Mr. S. Sriskandarajah who is now living in England has authored another worthy book. The first book, *The Ethical Essence of the Tamils*, a critical commentary on selected Tirukkural verses has proved his erudition and eminence in portraying the Tamil traditions and culture. The present work *Scenes from Tamil Classics* arises out of his love for the Tamil society, especially the youth and children whose exposure to Tamil remains limited. We are well aware of the present plight not only in other nations but in Tamil Nadu itself how the student community is plunging proudly into mastering universal English while shamelessly forgetting its glorious past and ancient Tamil classics.

In the opening chapters Mr. Sriskandarajah has attempted an illuminating introduction on the Tamil language, land, people, culture and their classics. It is a scholarly introduction. There he has stated the melancholic status of Sri Lankan Tamils. He has rightly classified the ancient, middle and modern period, and provided a short synopsis which serves as a good guide to Tamil literary history.

Any knowledge should be a universal possession; it should not be contained within national or other boundaries. All knowledge is the heritage of mankind and it belongs to all as of right. Several centuries before the birth of Christ, in the land of the Tamils in India, a literary tradition was stored in a treasury of living literature which has survived until to-day. Indian national poet Subramania Bharatiar, in one of his poems, speaks of what the Tamil people should do to advance the cause of their literature and culture. He directs them to make efforts to popularise Tamil culture and values, among the people of other lands. *We are the trustees of a rich heritage and it is our duty to share with the rest of the world the best that has been said and written by our forefathers* says the great linguistic scholar and translator the late Mr. J.V. Chelliah from Sri Lanka.

Today ancient Tamil literature has become a closed book even to educated people. An interest in it could be created by competent English translations of those classics. Mr. Sriskandarajah's present work, *Scenes from Tamil Classics*, is an admirable step in fulfilling this purpose. He has made a random selection of poems from classical Tamil literature such as Puranaanooru, Nattrinai, Kuruntokai, Kalittokai, Naaladiyar, the Tirukkural, the Naanmanikkadigai etc. He also has selected verses from the Thinaimaalai Noorraimbadu, the Kambaramayanam and also from Arichandra Puranam – a not so popular work - and a few verses from Avvaiyar and two unknown poets. His erudition in Tamil language and literature is well revealed in his elegant rendering of Saṅkam Classics which are aptly fitted with a background and introduction.

The selection is truly random, and gives an a-la-carte taste to the reader, especially to one who is being introduced to the rich repertoire of Tamil literature for the first time. Mr. Sriskandarajah has selected a vast canvas for his translation, including selections from Akam, Puram and didactic works on ethics.

The quality of translation by Mr. Sriskandarajah is uniformly good. He has made a faithful and at the same time a lucid, translation without sacrificing the English idiom or Tamil ethos. He has avoided paraphrasing and translated almost all the words in the text, so that one who wants to read the original, can do so with the help of the translation. His translation is beautifully plain, while maintaining the ancient flavour of Tamil verses. He has effectively used the blank-verse metre without rhyme for his translation. A good example is his beautiful translation of the Kurunthokai verse 'Yayum Gnayum' at page 75. Any lover of literature who chances to come across the verses will be struck by their beauty and charm and by their unique lyrical quality.

Poetry is essentially a medium for the communication of emotions. Many of the poems chosen for this book are excellent conveyors of genuine sentiments and thus contribute to great poetry. The dramatic narrative of a newly wedded wife serving her husband with tastefully cooked food and the husband savouring it is beautifully presented in the translation of verse No: 167 of Kurunthokai. The profound pathos of the sorrowing daughters of *Pari* the philanthropist, who had lost their father and land is rendered effectively in his translation of Puranaanooru Verse No: 112. The macabre scene of a valiant mother visiting the battlefield with a sword in hand, to verify whether her son died as a coward or a brave youth, is presented with all the powers of emotive poetry in his elucidation of Verse No: 278 of Purananooru.

What is most useful to the lay reader is the beautiful introductory note given by the author for each verse. It effectively explains the content of the poem and its setting and helps the reader to dive deep into the essence and beauty of the poem.

Scenes from Tamil Classics is a praise-worthy and remarkable effort, and will be very useful to any person who needs an introduction to the treasure of Tamil literature. I congratulate Mr. Sriskandarajah and wish him well in all his endeavours.

Dr. Avvai Natarajan

(Former Vice Chancellor – Tanjore Tamil University)

CHAPTER 1

A BRIEF HISTORY OF TAMIL LANGUAGE

A proper understanding of classical Tamil literature will be difficult without at least a brief knowledge of the history of the Tamils. Indologists now say that in prehistoric India a language called Proto Dravidian was in use. A foreign race of people called Aryans entered the land of India through the North Western Pass. Another race of people called 'Turanians' came into India through the North Eastern Pass. These two foreign races settled down in North India and mixed and mingled with the Proto Dravidians who were living in North India as well as South India. This intermingling, over a period of time, led to several changes and modifications in the language that was then spoken by the aboriginal Proto Dravidians in North India. These changes and modifications gave rise to languages such as Prakrit and Pali.

Even at that stage, in certain pockets of North India several corrupted dialects of the Proto Dravidian language were in use. Speakers of such corrupted Proto Dravidian dialects led a secluded life and this resulted in such Proto Dravidian dialects remaining in use for several centuries thereafter. This is the reason why several languages of North India such as Kolami, Parji, Naiki, Gondi, Ku, Kuvi, Konda, Malda, Orroan, Gadba, Khuruka and Brahui are still regarded as Dravidian languages. When the speakers of those languages came into closer contact with the speakers of Prakrit and Pali, the number of those speaking Kolami, Parji, Naiki etc. dwindled. Baluchistan is a region in West Pakistan whose people speak a language called Brahui which is rich in many Dravidian linguistic elements. Records reveal that in the census of 1911, Brahui was treated as a Dravidian language. It is reckoned that in 1911, about one hundred and seventy thousand (170,000) people spoke Brahui. Today this number has dwindled down to a few thousands only. From this it is evident that in the hoary past Dravidians were occupying lands extending from the North Western Pass to Bengal and that they were speaking Proto Dravidian.

Even now there are many similarities in terms of syntax between many North Indian languages and the Dravidian languages. This could be due to the fact that the North Indian languages borrowed and adopted many features that were special and peculiar to Proto Dravidian languages. Today, India is a sub continent of many races, ethnic groups, many faiths and languages, though it remains a secular state despite its Hindu majority population. Although many languages in ancient India had their own peculiar literature, over a period of time, due to the political superiority of the people to whom Sanskrit was the official and court language, Sanskrit became the official language for the whole of India and this in turn suppressed the development of other ancient languages and literature of India.

When we speak of Indian civilisation, it is pertinent to remember the words of Alan Danielou, the French linguist who translated the Tamil epic Cilappatikāram into English in the year 1968. He said: *"Many ancient legends and myths and much historical information that we know today only through Sanskritic versions came originally from non-Sanskritic sources. The great epics the Mahabharata and the Ramayana and the myths and tales compiled in the vast encyclopaedic works known as the Purāṇas (the ancient chronicles) probably belonged originally to other languages of India".*

When Prakrit and Pali gained ground in the North, the Proto Dravidian language was forced to take refuge in the South. In course of time, due to geographical and physical differences between the different regions in the South, even the Proto Dravidian language spoken in the South began to differ from county to county and province to province. The widening of this difference was augmented by the fact that transport facilities were poor in those days. The Dravidian language that was spoken in the deep South began to be called Tamil. The Dravidian language that was spoken in the area north of Tiruppati hills began to be called Telungu. The language spoken by the people in the Mysore area began to be called

Kannadam. The language spoken by the people who lived in the South Western region began to be called Malayalam. Of these four modified languages, Tamil is the language with a long literary heritage.

It was only at a very late stage that the other four languages of the South came to be referred to as "Dravidam". Dravidam is clearly a corruption of the word "Tamil". At some point in the history of South India, some people referred to Kannadam language as Karunāṭṭut Tamiḷ; "Thulu" language as Thulu Nāṭṭut Tamiḷ and "Malayalam" language as Malaināṭṭut Tamiḷ.

Notwithstanding the changes that have taken place in all these four main Dravidian languages, there could still be found many clear common features in these four languages. Dr.M.Varadarajan has explained these features extensively in his book entitled "History of Language". At least about five thousand words are common to these four Dravidian languages. Because of the heavy influx of words from Sanskrit, which is now a dead language like Latin, Kannadam and Telungu emerged as quite different and distinct languages about the sixth century AD. Until about 12th century there was not much difference between the Tamil language and the Malayaalam language. Before the 12th century, Tamil was the official language in the Malai Nādu or Malayalam region. The word "Kēraḷam" is a corruption of the word

"Cēraḷam". "Aḷam" in the Tamil language means land or region. Therefore Cēraḷam means the land or region of the Cērās. Cilappatikāram is an epic of the 3rd century AD. Iḷaṅkō Adikaḷ the author of Cilappatikāram was a person from Cēra Nādu whose current name is Kerala.

Tamil language is the official language of Tamil Nadu. It is in Tamil Nadu that there is a Ministry for Tamil language and Tamil affairs. Tamil is spoken in Sri Lanka, Burma, Singapore, Malaysia, Indonesia, South Africa, Fiji Islands and Mauritius. It is today spoken by about seventy-five million people all over the world.

The ethnic violence in Sri Lanka has compelled a good number of Sri Lankan Tamils to flee the country and they have taken refuge in countries such as Germany, France, Switzerland, Denmark, Netherlands, Norway, U.K, Canada, Australia, Italy, Sweden, Finland and the U.S.A.

CHAPTER 2

A SHORT HISTORY OF SRI LANKAN TAMILS

The Tamils of the modern Sri Lanka are believed to be the aborigines of Sri Lanka, though today they are living there as a minority group occupying the North and East of Sri Lanka. There are Tamils living in the central province of Sri Lanka also. They are refered to as upcountry Tamils and are the descendants of South Indian Tamils who were taken to Sri Lanka by the British Raj as indentured labourers to work in the tea and rubber plantations of the British Raj. “Lanka”, in the Sanskrit language means island. Historians now say that before Sri Lanka became an island, the present land mass of Sri Lanka was an integral part of South India.

Cilappatikāram, a Tamil epic of the second century A.D., refers to a deluge, during which a part of South India was submerged under the sea. Present Sri Lanka could be a part of the original South Indian land-mass that survived the deluge but got cut off from the mainland of South India. When that landmass became separated from the main landmass of South India, it was inhabited by Tamils or their predecessors called proto Dravidians. That is how this land mass came to be known as Lanka.

Tamils were Saivites, that is, worshippers of the Almighty Siva. In other words, the original religion that prevailed in Lanka was Saivism. This is the reason why the most ancient and pre-Buddhist shrines in Lanka happen to be Saivite shrines. The shrine in the east of modern Sri Lanka is a shrine for Lord Siva and is known as Tirukkuṇamalai (Erroneously called Tirukkoṇēswaram). Tirukkuṇamalai means sacred hill of the east. Even now the Sinhalese people call the area Tirukkuṇamalai. The shrine in the west of Lanka is known as Muṉṉeswaram; the shrine in the south is known as Katiramalai - also called Katirkāmam; the shrine in the north west is known as Tirukētīswaram; and the shrine in the north is known as Kīrimalai - also known as Nakulēswaram which is a Sanskritization of the Tamil word Kīrimalai.

Certain parts of Lanka became a Buddhist land only after the third century before Christ. With the spread of Buddhism in Lanka, many Tamils of Lanka also became Buddhists. The scriptures of Buddhism, the Tripitaka, were in the Pali language. The spread of Buddhism in Lanka resulted in many Pali words gaining currency among the Tamil speaking Buddhist population of Lanka. Gradually the Tamil language became so adulterated with Pali words that it gave birth to a new language called the Sinhalese language. It is estimated that more than thirty per cent of the Sinhalese language vocabulary is still Tamil. Devoid of its Aryan pretensions, the Sinhala language in its nakedness reveals that it is a derivative of the Tamil language with an admixture of Pali.

The rehashed Sinhala language owes its origin to Tamil language. This off-shoot is an amalgam of infiltration, adulteration and corruption of the language from which it is born. The first language that sprang up was the Sinhalese language.

Lanka was called Ceylon by the British. In 1972, the Sinhala government changed the name and Lanka assumed the new name of Sri Lanka. The Tamils, however still call it Ilaṅkai and write it as such.

In South India the original Tamil language gave birth to four major related languages. They are Kaṉṉadam, Teluṅgu, Malayāḷam and Tuḷu. These four became separate languages due to the Tamil language accepting Sanskrit words indiscriminately through North Indian contacts and conquests, as well as the influence of North Indian religions such as Jainism and Buddhism.

In the Vintaṉai area of the east of Sri Lanka there still lives an unrefined tribal group of people in the jungles. They live as hunters. These people are called *Vēdar* by the Tamils. The word *Vēdar* comes from the Tamil word *Vēdan. Vēdan* is a pure Tamil word meaning hunter. *Vēdar* is the plural form of the word *Vēdan.* Sinhalese call this uncivilised group of people the *Vettā. Vettā* is not a Sanskrit word nor is it a Pali word.

This lends support to the theory that Lanka has been a land of the Tamils from time immemorial.

Though the present day Sri Lankan Tamils had been the aborigines of Lanka, yet over the centuries, on many occasions, there have been many migrations from South India to Lanka. From the pre-Christian era, three main Tamil dynasties ruled South India. They were the Cōḻās, the Cērās and the Pāṇdiyās. In addition, there were feudal Lords or Barons loyal to the various dynasties. These dynasties were always at war with one another; so were the feudal lords. Whenever wars broke out between two dynasties or among the feudal lords, ordinary innocent citizens were the first casualties.

In the wake of wars, people were rendered refugees and many of them found the island of Lanka, which was only 18 miles away, a safe refuge; and they crossed the sea and started a new life there with their aboriginal Tamil brothers. In this way the aboriginal Tamil population of Lanka swelled due to the migration of Tamils into the island at different points of history from the mainland. Some of the place names in the Northern and Eastern provinces still bear testimony to this fact of immigration from South India from time to time.

CHAPTER 3

A Brief History of Tamil Literature

The greatness of a nation does not lie in her bricks and mortar, but rather in her colourful and splendid achievements in the area of art and literature.

Apart from Chinese, Tamil is the only example, in history, of an ancient classical language which has had an unbroken and voluminous literary record of a higher order covering a period of more than two thousand years. It has proudly survived as the spoken language of more than seventy five million people today. The vitality of the Tamil language has been preserved over the centuries and the words then used are still in use and are intelligible. An Englishman cannot today make out an Anglo Saxon text unless he has had good training and discipline in that field. But the language of the Tamil classics is not far removed from the language of today. Such is the robust nature of Tamil which has endured through the ages, and still remains resilient and young. This is the reason why recently Tamil has been recognised as a classical language.

The Tamil contribution to the totality of Indian civilisation and culture has been great. The earliest Tamil literature currently available is in verse form and contains an astonishing wealth of poetry. The themes of these poems are mainly love, war and ethics.

Classical Tamil literature is said to have been produced over a period of about a thousand years between the 5th century BC and the 5th century AD. It consists of the Eight Anthologies called the Eṭṭuttokai, the Ten Long Poems called the Pattuppāṭṭu, the Patiṉeṇkīḻkkaṇakku and a work of grammar called the Tolkāppiyam. Generally speaking, Tamil literature has a history of about two thousand five hundred years.

In the classical Tamil literature called Caṅkam Literature referred to above, there is no clear reference either to Kannadam or Telungu. This is because, literature in Kannadam and Telungu came into being only after 8th century AD. It needs no reiteration that Malayalam produced its literature much later than 8th century AD.

Up to the fourth century AD the Sanskrit language did not exert much influence on the Tamil language. When Buddhism and Jainism struck firm roots and spread to the Tamil speaking regions in the South, somewhere in the first century BC, the propagators of those North Indian protestant religions who were well versed in Sanskrit, Prakrit and Pali, besides being proficient in the Tamil language, started using non Tamil words to convey the religious concepts and philosophy of the invading religions. Gradually, in course of time, foreign words infiltrated the vocabulary of the Tamil language.

When Jainism and Buddhism struck root in the regions of the Tamils, many Tamil kings and Tamil scholars who were opposed to Brahminical practices were attracted by the atheistic philosophy and became converted to Buddhism and Jainism. This was the time when the age old dynasties of the Tamils, namely, the Cērās, the Cōḻās and the Pāṇdiyās were routed and forced out of power and the Tamil regions came under the suzerainty of a new dynasty called the Pallavās. Many Pallavā kings were well versed both in the Tamil and the Sanskrit languages. Some of them had a partiality for Sanskrit and professed Jainism.

The spread of Jainism and Buddhism adulterated the Tamil language, contaminated Tamil culture and changed the course of Tamil traditional way of life. However, it must be stressed that the spread of religions that were opposed to Saivaism willy-nilly produced a fertile climate for the creation of three great epics in the Tamil language, namely Cilappatikāram, Maṇimēkalai and Cīvakacintāmaṇi.

The literary history of Tamils used to be classified in many ways. But in my view, it is desirable to divide it into three periods namely the Ancient period, the Middle period and the Modern period.

The Ancient period may again be sub divided into the Caṅkam period, the period of Ethical Literature and the period of the Epics.

The Middle period could be divided into the following sub periods:

a) Period of devotional literature; (From 600 AD to 900AD)
b) Period of later epics, works of Grammar (such as Iṟaiyaṉār Kaḷaviyal), works of Cēkkiḻār, Kampar, Oṭṭakkūttar, Avvaiyār etc, and works of narrative poetic compositions (900 AD to 1200 AD).
c) Period of Commentaries (from 1200 AD to 1500AD)
d) Period of Puranic Literature (from 1500AD to 1800AD)

The Modern period covers the 19th and the 20th centuries which, as a result of printing facilities, have produced a great volume of literature unparalleled in the twenty-five centuries old literary history of the Tamils.

This small book is intended to include a few glimpses of the works of the Ancient period and the Middle period only, though references are also made to works of modern period here and there.

CHAPTER 4

TAMILS WERE NOT GREAT CHRONICLERS

Tamils were a great people; but they were not historians. This has been a great defect in their life. The failure to maintain a record of past events in the life of the Tamil people is inexplicable. As far as the ancient Tamils are concerned, even in relation to Tamil literature, there was a comparable failing in that the ancient Tamil poets failed to create literature that would last for the future as a record of the past. They don't appear to have felt the need for such complete and detailed lasting pieces of literature. At least until the 3rd century AD that appears to have been the trend of the Tamil poets.

During the dark centuries of Tamil history which the Indian historians describe as the Kalappra's period when the traditional Cērās, Cō<u>l</u>ās and Pāṇdiyās were driven out of power by the invaders from the North. This resulted in the neglect and disregard of Tamil literature and Tamil culture. At that time the humble Tamils realised the need for recorded history and the importance of preserving their literature in some permanent and enduring form. In the many centuries that preceded the dark centuries, there were great Tamil poets who possessed great capacity for composing several hundreds of love poems and war poems, but the need for conjoining the individual poems into a coherent garland never occurred to them.

From the mass of the poems that has been made available to us now by the untiring efforts of scholars like C. W. Thamotharam Pillai of Jaffna and Dr. U. V. Saminatha Iyer of South India, we now know that there lived in the Tamil land centuries ago a great Cōḻa king called Karikāl Vaḷavaṉ. His administrative skills and literary prowess were so great that he could have been made the hero of a great epic, if only the Tamils had had the yearning for making garlands out of individual poems. If Karikālaṉ had been a king of any other country in the West, say Rome or Athens or Sparta, there would have come into being many epics centering on him. By their very nature, such epics would have spread far and wide and survived all natural and physical disasters, and would have served as a great source of Tamil history. The information about king Karikālaṉ, which we are able to gather in dribs and drabs from various single poems, lends weight to such a supposition.

Like Karikālaṉ of the Cōḻa dynasty, there lived many eminent kings in the Cēra and the Pāṇdiya dynasties also. However there is no epic literature featuring them as its heroes that might have enabled us to learn in detail about them, their administration, or about the status of Tamil Nadu during their times.

There were many philanthropists too who lived exemplary lives worthy of emulation. For example Pāri, Kāri, Aay, Eḻili, Naḷḷi and Pēkan were great philanthropists and feudal Lords. There are many individual poems in the Eṭṭuttokai and the Pattuppāṭṭu singing their praises and excellences. However there is no single work of literary art in the form of an epic extolling the greatness of those philanthropists; if there were they would have enabled us to learn of their lives and times and to bask in the glory of the ancient Tamils.

If a person of Pāri's munificence or eminence or of Pēkan's boundless liberality had been born in another clime, he would have become the hero of many an epic. In the known history of Tamil literature there lived a poet called Kapilar who lived and died for the philanthropist Pāri of the Paṟampu Malai. But there is no continuous or narrative work of Tamil literature for us to know more about their friendship or about the noble life they led.

Ancient Tamils had everything; but their contentment restrained them from giving a thought to the future. In their individual poems they recorded their inner feelings as they felt them. They did not have the mind to solder those individual flowers of poems into a garland using a little bit of solder called exaggerations and pleasant lies. They failed to realise that stories are catchy and that humans are fond of living in a fool's paradise.

There lived in the Tamil land, poets of the calibre of Homer or Valmiki or Kalidas. But those Tamil poets did not care to create epics of the kind Valmiki, Homer or Kalidas created. Why?

We may attempt to give reasons, but that will not satisfy the present day Tamils. Had the Tamils created such epics of great grandeur making Karikālaṉ or Cēran Ceṅkuṭṭuvaṉ or Pāri or Paraṇar or Kapilar as the hero of their epics, the Tamil literature which is the oldest and the richest living literature of India today, would have come to be recognised as the greatest living literature of the world and the Tamils would have earned acknowledgement as a great race in consequence. But that was not to be. If the Tamils had composed epics, the Encyclopaedia Britanica and the American Encyclopaedia would have then defined Tamils as the most ancient race endowed with the noblest literature and cultural heritage instead of describing the Tamils, as they do now, as the "greatest temple builders".

We know not who first formed the opinion that it was not enough to compose single individual poems about a single incident in a person's life, but that there should be poems of a continuous nature narrating their life and times. But we gather from the extant literature that is vouchsafed to us that there were two poets who thought about the need for it and did something concrete. They were Iḷaṅkō Adikaḷ and Cāttaṉār.

Iḷaṅkō Adikaḷ composed the Cilappatikāram and Pulavar Cāttaṉār gave us the Maṇimēkalai. It is said that Cilappatikāram has Jainistic flavour while the Maṇimēkalai smacks of Buddhist philosophy. Be that as it may. Iḷaṅkō Adikaḷ and Cāttaṉār broke new grounds and paved the way for other epics and, in the centuries that followed them, we were blessed with the Cīvakacintāmaṇi by Tiruttakka Tēvar and Kamparāmāyaṇam by Kampaṉ.

How was it that Iḷaṅkō Adikaḷ and Cāttaṉār could achieve that which Kapilar and Paraṇar of the Caṅkam age could not achieve? It is not easy to explain. Kapilar and Paraṇar had feelings and imagination, but they thought only of their contemporary life; they did not think of the future. As for Iḷaṅkō and Cāttaṉār, they had not only poetic feelings and imagination, they had some vision of the future also; they had some aims and objectives too. From his introductory verses, it is clear that Iḷaṅkō must have felt that the following matters, namely (1) the greatness of Kaṇṇaki as embodiment of love and chastity, (2) the belief of the Tamils that unjust administration will have inevitable consequences, (3) the inescapability of Karma and (4) his experience of the world and the condition of the Tamils of his time should be made known to the outside world. This objective was true with Cāttaṉār also. Cāttaṉār wanted to let the world know of the great sacrifice and service performed by Maṇimēkalai, daughter Kōvalaṉ and Mātavi in propagating the great teachings of Lord Buddha who was born a Hindu. This resulted in the birth of the Maṇimēkalai epic. The Cilappatikāram and the Maṇimēkalai are the oldest surviving epics of the Tamils. These two epics are referred to as the twin Tamil epics *(Iraṭṭaikkāppiyaṅkaḷ).*

The Tamil world of today should be happy and content that at least these works have been vouchsafed to posterity, and that they are able to feel proud of their ancient literary heritage, which speaks volumes of their noble culture and civilization. Even so it is much regretted that our forbears had failed to leave a continuous record of their past history as the Western countries have done. We never care to ask today whether we ourselves are free from such criminal charges today, given that we are better equipped than our forbears were to record history in a systematic way.

It is master pieces like Puṟanāṉūṟu and Patiṟṟuppattu that give us an insight into the character and achievements of the Tamil people. The extant classical literature was not all that our forbears produced. There would have been numerous poems other than those that are available to us as the Eṭṭuttokai, the Pattuppāṭṭu and the Patiṉeṇkīḻkkaṇakku. The collectors and selectors of these poems will have been aware of many other poems containing historical information about the Tamils. The ancient editors of such anthologies perhaps chose only those poems that appealed to them. The editors' choice, of course, would have been in line with their interests; anything that touched on subjects outside their purview would not have found a place in their anthology. If the selector had no interest in history, he would have rejected poems of historical narration. In the same way, another compiler who had no sense of music will have excluded compositions in verse which contained details of music and musicians of the past. Equally, want of time and lack of skill will have contributed to the omission of quite a number of poems. These factors will have led the ancient editors to limit the anthologies to four hundred verses only. (Puṟanāṉūṟu, Akanāṉūṟu, Paḻamoḻi Nāṉūṟu etc.)

It is also possible that the poems which are included in the anthologies were the only ones which were available to the editors at that time, the rest having been lost to deluge, conflagration, and insects. Who knows?

The sombre thought that it would have been nice if those editors had been less fussy in making their selection haunts everyone today. How much more authentic information about the life of the Tamils might have been preserved in the poems which the editors possibly rejected?

While we lament the possibility, we are also sadly reminded of the fact that even the extant classical literature is not totally complete. Let me illustrate. Poem No. 234 of Naṟṟiṇai is missing completely; part of poem number 385 is also not there. Poems Nos 129 and 130 of Aiṅkuṟu Nūṟu have been lost while poems Nos 416 and 490 are incomplete. The Patiṟṟuppattu is also not complete. Instead of 100 poems, we have only 80 poems.

At the time of compilation there were seventy poems in Paripādal. However now we have only 33 of them. The remaining 37 poems have been lost.

In Puṟanāṉūṟu, poems No.267 and No.268 have disappeared mysteriously. The beginning lines of poems Nos. 328 and 370 are not there. The ending lines of poems numbers 244, 355 and 361 are not there. In addition, in about 40 Puṟanāṉūṟu poems a few lines are missing here and there.

Despite all these shortcomings in the classical anthologies, we are able to breathe a sigh of relief that we are fortunate enough to have at least what we now have.

In the pages that follow we will see some of the poetic paintings contained in the body of the literature referred to above, which are gleanings from the glorious Tamil classics.

CHAPTER 5

PANORAMIC SCENES IN TAMIL LITERATURE

Episode 1

CANNOT WE UNITE AGAINST OUR ARCH ENEMY?

As I thumbed through the pages of Puṟanāṉūṟu, a poem by Kōvūr Kiḻār giving advice to two Cōḻa kings called Nalam Kiḷḷi and Nedum Kiḷḷi directed my thoughts back to Tamil Eelam and made me long to have today in our midst a person of Kōvūr Kiḻār's sagacity and reverence. My yearning did not stop at that. It carried me to yet another world of practical wisdom, forcing me to ponder over the mature advice Tiruvaḷḷuvar has bequeathed to us in one of his Kuṟaḷs in the chapter on Ministers. He writes as follows: "He is the able Minister who is endowed with the tactical ability to disunite allies, to cherish and maintain existing relationships and friendships, and to unite those that have become estranged".

A critical perusal of Puṟanāṉūṟu poems will not fail to reveal that a good many of the Caṅkam poets acted as such Ministers during occasions of crisis, and the kings had great respect and regard for such well-meaning poets since they were devoid of partisanship. The forty-fifth poem in Puṟanāṉūṟu depicts an instance that merits attention. The author of the poem is Kōvūr Kiḻār. This is a poem addressed to two Cōḻa kings – Nalam Kiḷḷi and

Nedum Kiḷḷi. Nedum Kiḷḷi was constantly at war with Nalam Kiḷḷi. Their constant fights and wars caused untold hardships to the people. Besides, it was causing irreparable damage to the reputation of the Cōḻa Dynasty and encouraging the kings of the Cērā Dynasty and the Pāṇdiyā Dynasty to attack the Cōḻā. When Nedum Kiḷḷi was ruling the city of Āvūr, Nalam Kiḷḷi marched to that city and besieged Nedum Kiḷḷi inside the fort. Kōvūr Kiḻār requested Nedum Kiḷḷi to come out and fight Nalam Kiḷḷi. Not having the mind to engage in a bloody war, Nedum Kiḷḷi conceded defeat, surrendered the city of Āvūr and left for the city of Uṟaiyūr to live there peacefully.

Not content with conquering Āvūr, Nalam Kiḷḷi set out once again and marched on to Uṟaiyūr. This unconscionable act on the part of Nalam Kiḷḷi caused deep concern in the mind of the poet Kōvūr Kiḻār. The poet feared that the internecine feud between the two kings of the Cōḻa Dynasty might spell its doom. Thus he decided to appeal to the two kings in the following terms:

"The person who is opposing you is not a Cēra king who sports the white flower of the palmyrah palm as the symbol of his dynasty. Nor is he a Pāṇdiya king whose dynasty symbol is the neem flower. Your garland is made of Ātti flower. Your opponent's garland too is made of Ātti flower. In other words he belongs to the same lineage as you do. Whoever is the loser in the battle, it is the Cōḻa

Dynasty which will be the loser. It is not possible for you both to win the war. If one wins, the other will lose. Therefore what you are now doing does not become your great family. It will only make your opponents revel and rejoice. Please therefore refrain from fighting."

History has it that Nalam Kiḷḷi and Nedum Kiḷḷi heeded the advice of poet Kōvūr Kiḻār and refrained from engaging in internecine and self-destructive fighting. What a salubrious effect it would have on the Eelam Tamils, if only they had in their midst a person of Kōvūr Kiḻār's stature. Then the warring factions of the Eelam Tamils all of whom are claiming to be waging a war of independence against the Sinhalese majority could be reconciled and become a solid force to be reckoned with! Now we see the poem in translation.

He does not sport the palmyra flower,
Nor does he wear the neem;
You sport the Ātti flower,
And so does the one with whom you fight.
Whichever one of you is vanquished,
it is your whole community that suffers.
There cannot be two victors.
So what you are bent upon
will not serve the interests of your people.
If the two of you fight with each other,
that will only encourage your enemies round about.

(Puṟanāṉūṟu - 45)

Episode 2

WE ARE ALSO MADE REFUGEES

Nature is at times very cruel; at least it appears to be so. Over the years, poets across the world have drawn our attention to this naked truth. "Even the fabulously rich who once rode on elephants, seated under protective umbrellas, could become destitute and migrate on foot, deserting their homestead in search of refuge and asylum". Thus said the poet Ativīrarāma Pāṇdiyaṉ.

The other day when I was at the Acton Town Hall, watching a programme of cultural activities organised in aid of the Sri Lankan Tamil Orphans, I chanced to meet two boys whom I had known in Jaffna. The boys belonged to a family of Paramparai Paṇakkārar (hereditarily rich family). That family was known for its nobility and generosity also.

Obviously, in Jaffna, these two boys lived in comfort and luxury. When I saw these boys at the Acton Town Hall, devoid of all the comforts and cheer which they used to enjoy, my heart sank into my shoes. Asked where their parents were, they replied that they were shot to death by the Indian Army in 1988, that their kith and kin were exterminated by the Sinhalese army and that they had only managed to flee to London by the grace of a family friend.

While I was returning home, the excruciating experiences of these two children occupied my mind. As my imagination played on their situation, I remembered a poetic painting in a Puṟanāṉūṟu verse.

The verse is about Pāri of Paṟampu hills. Pāri was the chieftain of a mountainous county known as Paṟampu which comprised three hundred villages. Pāri was noted for his wealth as well as his philanthropy.

The Pāṇḍiyās, the Cērās and the Cōḻās were envious of Pāri. As none of them could singly take him on, the three joined hands treacherously, killed him and destroyed his county, leaving his two daughters, Aṅkavai and Caṅkavai, helpless and destitute.

The children were shocked and shattered. The chieftains and barons of other counties who had once supported Pāri, refused to give protection or refuge to the orphaned children, fearing that the wrath of the three kings might fall on them.

Poet Kapilar who was a great friend of Pāri took charge of Pāri's daughters; but he had difficulty in consoling them. A few weeks later, the two children were seen standing outside the hut of Kapilar. It was night time. They were aimlessly and vacantly gazing at the moon which was full.

One of the girls suddenly started to weep. She was reminded of the nights they had spent with their father, watching the same moon. She lamented and compared the two situations, the situation only a month ago when their father was alive, and the present situation when their father was no more. These children portrayed their mental anguish in a poem: "*Only a month ago we without a care enjoyed the beautiful sight of this full moon. Then our father was alive, and our county free. Today again we see the same moon, but we are not in the same mood and don't enjoy its beauty. The greedy kings have taken our county and its beautiful hills. We are now countyless and fatherless, real refugees.*"

The children of Pāri, known as Aṅkavai and Caṅkavai, lamented in that way two thousand years ago. That was not a frequent occurrence then.

Today, every other Eelam Tamil child appears to have the same story to narrate, but nobody seems to be prepared to describe their anguish even in prose, let alone in verse.

Let us now see the verse from Puṟanāṉūṟu in translation.

Last month this moon shone bright and clear;

then our father was alive

and our hills were not in the hands of foreigners.
This month the same moon shines;
but the plundering kings have seized our hills
and made us orphans.

(Pu̱ranā̱nū̱ru -112)

Episode 3

THE HEROIC MOTHER

An old woman was at home minding her own business even at her ripe age. She was so old that the veins stood out on her hollow and shrunken shoulders. She was eagerly expecting her only son, who had gone to war with his comrades, to return victorious. Time ticked away; but there was no sign of his return. Instead there came rumours that unable to face the attack of the foe, her son had turned his back and fled from the battle-field. This was the last thing she expected to hear of her son, whom she had all these years believed to be valiant and brave. The unpleasant rumours sent shock waves coursing through her fragile body. Her sense of shame and honour now took control of her, and her wrath blazed out. She vowed thus: "If what I hear be true; if from the shock of battle my son has shrunk, I shall cut off these breasts of mine that gave him suck."

So saying, with sword in hand, she went to the battlefield in search of her son who allegedly had brought shame and disgrace to her family and country. At the field of battle which was red with the gore of the dead she turned over every dead body searching for her son. At last she saw her son's mangled corpse with all its limbs severed by the sword.

At that moment her joy knew no bounds. The fact that her son was dead and that she had become destitute did not occur to her. The fact that the rumours she heard had been proved untrue gave her such immense pleasure that her heart rejoiced far more than it did on the day she gave birth to him.

Such was the hallmark of Tamil womanhood two thousand years ago. Those of us who had the benefit of learning Tamil literature when we were young found it difficult to believe that there could have been mothers of such valour and bravery that they treasured their motherland more than their own possessions, including their own blood and bone. But the events in Tamil Eelam during the last twenty-five years have proved beyond doubt that we have to believe every word of what is contained in Tamil literature.

Now, have a look at the Puṟanāṉūṟu poem which portrays the scene I have paraphrased in the foregoing lines.

Her veins stood out on her shrunken shoulders,
and her stomach looked like a lotus leaf,
she was so old and thin.
News came that on the battlefield
her son could not face the enemy
and turned his back.

Burning with anger, she made a vow:
"If like a coward
my son has turned his back,
I shall cut off the breasts
that gave him suck!"
Then with sword in hand, she searched the battlefield
drenched in blood.
When she found the body of her son hacked to pieces,
she was happier by far
than on the day when he was born.

(Puṟanāṉūṟu -278)

Episode 4

ANCIENT TREATMENT FOR GREY HAIR

We are luxuriating in a technological world which has mastered the cosmetic art of concealing grey hair and even baldness. Though it is a relief to hundreds of thousands of us, yet it is only a temporary solution. Almost two thousand years ago there lived in Tamil Nadu an eminent poet called Picirāntayār who has taught us not the art of concealing grey hair, but the secret of preventing greying altogether.

Picirāntayār was a poet of great consequence. He is said to have lived for more than a century free from all physical and mental afflictions. One day a group of connoisseurs of literature from an adjoining province visited him, having heard of his literary profundity and punditry. As they had heard of his ripe age, they had pictured him in their mind as a hunchback, with snowy hair. When they saw him face to face, they were shocked to see an upright and cheerful gentleman sporting a pitch black tuft of hair on his head. As that was a time when the Tamil people did not know of the European art of dying the hair, the visitors had no reason to doubt that his hair was truly black. So, after the social exchange of pleasantries, the visitors quietly approached the poet and enquired how it was possible for him to keep his black hair even after one hundred years. Picirāntayār, who had answered similar questions in the past, seated his admirers and explained the secret of his healthy and contented life. This is what he said:

"The youthfulness of the body depends on the wholesomeness of the mind. As long as the mind does not become fatigued, the body also will not become tired. If the mind gets tired, the body also will get tired. Grey hair and wrinkled skin are signs indicating that the mind is diseased. To this day my mind has not become exhausted or diseased. There are many reasons for that. They include domestic reasons as well as other reasons. If you ask me about my domestic past, my wife and children are endowed with wisdom coupled with a fund of affable qualities. Those who associate with me also conduct themselves in such a way as to make everybody happy. As for the country I live in, the ruler of the country is fair and just. To crown it all, in my country there live many great souls who are service-minded and free from all passions. To cut a long story short, it is due to the existence of a flawless family, peaceful country, a just ruler and great sages that I am able to maintain this state of health and composure".

The story narrated above is contained in a verse included in the anthology called Pur̲anān̲ūr̲u. Let us now see the translation of the verse.

"Your years are many, we have heard,
yet not a hair of your head is grey;
what is your secret?"
you ask me wondering.
My noble wife is virtuous
our children are well brought up
my servants give no cause for complaint
my king too protects his citizens;
Above all, my town is full of learned men
with all their passions quenched
humble and modest in all their ways".

(Puṟanāṉūṟu -191)

Episode 5

THE INSEPARABLE WIFE

"Love" and "lovers" are words that are freely bandied about and have been rendered empty and trite these days. True love however, that many-splendoured thing, will always be there as long as there are genuine lovers.

A Tamil poem from the anthology called Puṟanāṉūṟu portrays the throbbing anguish and fervent wishes of a dedicated true lover.

There lived a couple who were true lovers, who believed in karma and rebirth and wished to be man and wife in all their births. They were dutiful and honourable citizens. Invasion of their homeland by the rapacious enemy forces forced the husband into the battlefield of his own volition. Many weeks passed; he did not return; messages came confirming that he had become a martyr. The wife rushed to the battlefield and found his body, mortally wounded in the chest. She sobbed and cried until she lost her voice. The thought that she had been made destitute overnight wrenched her heart and made her feel helpless and hopeless. Simultaneously, the overriding thought that her husband had given up his life not for anything but for the defence and liberation of her motherland and homeland from the shackles of the invading enemy gave her great comfort.

Her thoughts flashed back, and the sweet and the not-so-sweet memories of her married life with her husband came to her mind in successive flashes. The ancient poem under consideration succinctly paints her feelings by means of an analogy and simple anecdote.

Wall lizards are domestic creatures in Sri Lanka and India. Some of them are destined to live in strange places like the axle or spokes of a cart which is drawn by oxen. When such a cart, with a lizard perilously perched on one of its spokes, sets off on a journey lasting many long days, one can imagine the number of rotations the wheel will make and the ups and downs the lizard will be subjected to. The wheel may rattle along rocky roads or wade through miry lanes, exposing the lizard to all manner of shocks, jerks, jolts and deafening noises. Willy-nilly the lizard hangs on in trepidation, firmly clinging to the spoke until the wheel ceases to rotate when the journey is over.

The weeping widow compares her life to the life of such a lizard. She had lived with her husband like the lizard on the spoke of the wheel, experiencing mutually shared pain and pleasure. As she had lived with her husband for many years, participating in all the ups and downs of life, she did not wish to be parted from him even when the vital spark of life had left him. So she goes to the maker of urns that are used for the burial of the dead and tells him that she needs an urn for the burial of her husband. But she asks that it is made a little larger so that her dead body could also be placed alongside his when she is dead too in a couple of days!

Lovers of today may have reservations about the wisdom of that noble and exemplary widow; but the moral of the poem is a mirror of the time, the classical era of the Tamils.

Potter, oh potter!
With him I have come through many a tight spot
like a little white lizard
hugging the spoke of a cart wheel.
But now he is gone.
Be kind, I beg you, and make me an urn,
to bury his ashes in this wide earth.
And, you potter, maker of urns for this old town,
make it big enough to hold my ashes too.

(Pu̲ranān̲ūr̲u - 256)

Episode 6

A MATTER OF HONOUR

Torture of the vanquished at the hands of the victor in battle is tragically all too commonplace. That this practice obtained even during the golden era of the Caṅkam Tamils is attested in a classical poem in the anthology of ancient poems called Puṟanāṉūṟu (collection of war poems). While we are rightly ashamed and humbled to hear from Puṟanāṉūṟu that some, at least, of our forebears perpetrated similar inhumanities upon their captives, some noble traditions treasured by the Tamils of the pre-Christian era are also communicated to us by the same poem.

The Cērās (ancient rulers of the present state of Kerala) and the Cōḻās (the ancient rulers of the present Tanjore and Trichy areas) were perpetually at war with each other. During one such war, a Cērā king known as Cēramāṉ Kaṇaikkāl Irumpoṟai was defeated and taken captive by a Cōḻa king called Cōḻaṉ Ceṅkaṇṇāṉ. As is to be expected, the Cēra king was imprisoned. However the Cēra king preferred instant death to humiliating imprisonment. The instantaneous, but final deliverance of the cyanide capsule was not then known to man, and was not therefore available to the Cēra king! In the prison cell, the captured king was subjected to ignominy, deprivation and persecution which are the lot of the Tamil boys and girls in the Sinhala prisons of Sri Lanka today. The Cēra king was denied not only food, but even water. After long weeks of denial, when the very feeling of thirst had atrophied, he was grudgingly offered a little water. But he refused the water. His proclivity for poetry instantly gave birth to a poem, the contents of which have continued to inspire and serve as a guiding light for generations of Tamils. It also vividly recounts the taunts and humiliations he experienced during his incarceration.

The vanquished king rejected the water and replied: "No, I will not drink this water even if my rejection of it means certain death to me. You silly gaolers may not know the traditions of the clan I belong to, but it is worth my spelling them out to you. I belong to a clan of kings who expect every child to be bold and brave, so much so that even when a child is still-born or even if born prematurely and with tenuous prospects of life, we do not deem such a child a non-entity. We will deem such a child also to be a live child and put it to the sword to give it a warrior's death. When such is the honour we attach to children of our clan, do you think that I, a king of the Cēra dynasty, held on one end of a chain like a dog and treated so cruelly by your mean officials, will beg you for a drop of water because of the thirst in my belly, and lap up a beggar's drink. No, never. I would rather die of thirst, than drink your water like a dog."

Let us now have a look at the translation of the Pur̲anāṉūr̲u poem in question.

If a child of my family should die,
or if it were born dead,
a mere lump of flesh,
not yet a human being,
they will put it to the sword,
to give it a warrior's death.
So would a king bring a son into this world
and keep him like a dog on a chain?
Or to assuage the fire in his belly,
would he have to beg for a drop of water,
or take his drink like a beggar
from the hands of cruel jailers?

(Pur̲anāṉūr̲u - 74)

Episode 7

UNFAIR TAXATION

Poem number 184 of Puṟanāṉūṟu depicts the pitiable plight of inconsiderate rulers who impose heavy taxation on their citizens, little realising that such an unwise course of action will spell their own doom.

During the Puṟanāṉūṟu time there lived a Pāṇdiyaṉ king called Pāṇdiyaṉ Aṟivudai Nampi. He was also a talented poet. He was the ruler of a country whose soil was very fertile. The country enjoyed regular rainfall making the landscape always verdant and green. Everyone was engaged in farming and the land yielded produce commensurate with the efforts put in. Mother Earth was happy that there was no soul who was complaining that they did not have enough to eat.

Though the people contributed more than their mite for the food resources of the country, the king little realised that the enviable food stock thus produced was due to the ever increasing effort of his people. People did their duty unfailingly, but he failed to perform his functions as a ruler properly. He spent more than he should. As far as the king was concerned he spent more than he received as dues, taxes, rents and rates from the people. When he found it difficult to make ends meet, he hit upon the undesirable plan of taxing his people heavily. His ministers advised him that the course he had embarked upon was capable of producing disastrous results and that he should desist from the plan he had proposed to put in place. They referred him to the wise words of Tiruvaḷḷuvar in the great Tirukkuṟaḷ and pointed out to him that there was no harm in one's avenues of income being narrow as long as the avenues of expenditure are not wider.

Their words fell on deaf ears. He went ahead with his proposed plan of increasing the taxes. The people became disenchanted. They lost interest in life. They began to feel that there was no point in their working hard if at the end of the day they were not going to be better off. When the per capita income fell, the produce of the land also fell and the treasury of the king showed signs of depletion. Instead of investigating the reason for the depletion of the treasury with a view to remedying the situation, and instead of tracing the root cause for the malady of depletion, he went on increasing the tax payable by the people.

The burden of taxation became unbearable but the people were reluctant to complain fearing that they might be singled out for punishment on possible trumped up charges of rebellion. As the king happened to be a person who respected and regarded people with literary prowess, the people approached a learned poet called Picirāntayār and pleaded with him to intervene on their behalf. The poet who was himself thoroughly frustrated with the way the king was acting, was now fortified in his belief that it was high time for him to tell the king "enough is enough" and that he should heed the views of the people.

Picirāntayār proceeded to the palace and announced his arrival. The king himself came to the palace gate to receive the scantily–clothed and white-bearded Picirāntayār. After seating the poet in the visitors' lounge and exchanging pleasantries, the king asked the poet whether he could be of any help to him. The poet did not want to state the purpose of his mission abruptly, so he said that he had come with a verse he had composed after witnessing a scene on a farm in the king's domain. He added that he in fact wanted the king to share the feelings he had put into the poem but that he could not find the opportune time to visit the palace earlier. Being a lover of literature and art himself, the king grew anxious and restless and requested the poet to recite the poem and elucidate its meaning.

The poet paused for a while and told the king that he would recite the poem and expatiate upon it after narrating an interesting incident which prompted the poem. The poet began:

"A couple of months ago I had occasion to go to Māṉā Maturai to attend a seminar near the mouth of the river Vaikai. My trip involved passing through wood lands. A scene I saw there gripped my mind so much that I wished to describe the scene vividly to you. However I could not find the time.

Once again, last week I chanced to go to Māṉā Maturai to attend the wedding of my grand-daughter. I passed through the same woodlands in the hope that I would be able to please my eyes with the sight of full-grown ears of the paddy plants. The sight I saw there made my heart sink. I saw about a dozen elephants trampling those beautiful paddy fields. The wild elephants did not stay in one place in the paddy field, but were roaming about eating the paddy all over the place. What they destroyed by their trampling and mischief was far greater than what they in fact needed. The devastation caused to the paddy field was such that those very elephants will find no point in visiting the plantation again as they had not left anything intact. Instead of the elephants having been allowed to go on a rampage into the field, if the paddy crop had been cut in small quantities and fed to the elephants at regular intervals, what was available in that field would have been sufficient to feed all those elephants for at least twelve months. Because the elephants ran amuck and trampled the field, there is now nothing left in it.

You may wonder why I thought it useful to narrate this incident. If by now you have not understood let me now tell you openly. It is generally thought by the citizens of your country that you are behaving in the same way as the elephants I just now described. If the taxes you levy from the people are reasonable and affordable, the people will continue to pay the taxes ungrudgingly and they will feel happy. On the other hand if you tax them beyond the level which they can afford, you will push them into poverty and they will not be able to pay you anything at all. They might even attempt to revolt against you. Such a state of affairs would not be desirable. Therefore it appears to me that you should forthwith announce a reduction in the tax rate. As you are a lover of poetry, let me recite that poem now. The poet recited the poem and glanced at the king to see his reaction. The king wiped his tears and clasped the hand of the poet signalling that he would do the needful at once. Here is that verse.

If only the ripe paddy is cut and rolled into balls,
even the yield of a plot of land less than an acre in size
will be enough to feed an elephant for many days.
But if the elephant were let loose in a field ten times the size,
it would destroy with its feet far more than it could ever eat.
So if a king is wise, and levies taxes that are fair and just,
he will raise millions of pounds and his country will enjoy great prosperity.
But if he is weak and thoughtless and surrounded by jabbering courtiers
who are nothing but foolish flatterers,
and if he is bent on extorting the most that he can get,
like the elephant let loose in the paddy field,
he will starve and bring his country to ruin.

(Pu̱ranāṉūṟu 184)

Episode 8

HIS BEARD IS STILL SOFT

There was a time when some of the stories we glean from the heroic poems of the Tamil classical period were hard to believe, though our mentors unsuccessfully tried to convince us that the stories portrayed by those poems were in essence true and not mere poetic imaginations or exaggerations. During the fifties, our Sinhalese brethren, blissfully forgetting that the Sri Lankan Tamils also have equal right to the country and its resources rode roughshod over the meek and gullible Tamils of Sri Lanka. Consequently I have had occasion to recall and ruminate on the classical period of the Cērās, the Cōḻās and the Pāṇḍiyās revealed through Tamil classical literature popularly referred to as Caṅkam literature.

Though received wisdom has it that history does repeat itself, I have nevertheless yearned for part at least of that ancient Tamil history to be re-enacted sooner in the Tamil soil of Sri Lanka. But at that time, the traditionally soft and humble Tamils of Tamil Eelam could not, all of a sudden, shake off their innate, inherited and ingrained gentleness, which had been nourished and cultivated over centuries of cultured life. It was impossible for them to become brutal and ruthless though the Sinhala tyranny and oppression demanded it urgently. However the intransigence, the fanaticism and the recurring duplicity of the successive chauvinistic Sinhala governments compelled the Tamils to become what they never wanted to become. So, from the late nineties we find the dramas and episodes painted vividly in the Puṟanāṉūṟu poems being re-enacted in the soil of Tamil Eelam.

The inimitable courage displayed by the indomitable Tamil youths during the much flaunted but most shameful "Operation Yāḻdēvi" by the Sri Lankan armed forces took me back to the pre-Christian era and revived the memory of a young warrior. The story of that warrior has been encapsulated in a poem attributed to a poet called Poṉmudiyār. It is the story of a young lad who still had only the rudiments of a beard, a boy in his early teens. The poet, who had known the boy from his childhood and had the chance of witnessing his prowess and performance on the battlefield, has picturesquely painted the metamorphosis of the young lad into a committed boy warrior.

It was reported in the Sri Lankan press at that time that hundreds of Tamil teenagers had lost their lives during the "Operation Yāḻdēvi" launched by the Sri Lankan armed forces. It is sad that the Tamil youths who are capable of achieving still greater things should be forced by the heartless Sinhalese government to lay down their lives like this. But then, how else can the Tamils redeem their honour and self-respect and live in peace. There were poets like Poṉmudiyār to sing the praise of those youths who gave their lives for the sake of their land and liberty. Who is there now in Tamil Eelam (except poet laureate Putuvai Rattinaturai), to eulogise the greatness and the sacrifice of the Tamil youths who became martyrs during "Operation Yāḻdēvi"? They gave their lives and many more of them continue to do so so that other suffering Tamils could live in peace and dignity in the years to come.

Here is a translation of that poem.

Oh my heart, you sorrow for this lad
who once cowered from the stick lifted in mock anger,
when he refused a drink of milk.
Now he is not content with killing elephants with spotted trunks;
this son of the doughty warrior who fell in battle yesterday,
seems unaware of the arrow in his own wound.
With his head of hair plumed like a horse's,
he has fallen on his shield.
Yet his beard is still soft.

(Puṟanāṉūṟu -310)

Episode 9

A CITIZEN'S DUTY

We live in a world where the young and the old clamour for rights and powers. Young children in this country demand that they should have the right even to divorce from their parents. Old and sickly men in the Western world demand that they should be at liberty to resort to euthanasia. Plants and animals also, through their human representatives, are deemed to have such and such rights. Scientists also put forward their share of the demand by clamouring that they should have the right to experiment with test tube babies and cloning. Seemingly, all these demands appear to make a mockery of the whole of human life and reduce humanity to nothingness.

When I reflected on the ethics and propriety of these demands, I remembered a classical poem in the Puṟanāṉūṟu in which a poet gives a list of duties which should be honoured and carried out by the members of the family. Conspicuously that poem did not spell out rights and powers!

Readers may or may not agree with what the poet said at a time when the social set up was quite different from what it is today. Though they may not agree with what is contained in the poem in its entirety, yet they may agree that the "ship of family" cannot steer smoothly unless each member of the family takes upon himself or herself the duty which he or she can perform most ably, and at the same time refrains from demanding rights and powers. It is salubrious to note that the poem in question was composed by a woman poet called Poṉmudiyār.

The poem may not appear to have relevance to the Tamil community living in the Western world as second class citizens or refugees. Certainly the Tamil world has come full circle since the days of the Caṅkam age, and it would appear that the duties listed in the poem now have great relevance to the Tamil society in the North and East of Sri Lanka. Every mother in Jaffna and Mannar, Kandy, Batticaloa and Trincomalee and Kilinochchi and Vanni feels that it is her duty to bring forth and rear valiant sons, and every young man and young woman in the Tamil soil of Sri Lanka feel that it is their duty to die for their freedom, land and language. The only difference is that a Puṟanāṉūṟu mother wanted to give birth to valiant sons only. But a Tamil Eelam mother feels strongly that both her male and female children should be chivalrous and valiant to be able to carry arms to vanquish the enemy who engages in the genocide of the Tamils. Now read the poem.

My duty is to bring forth and rear a son,
his father's is to make him noble,
the blacksmith's is to make him a spear,
the king's to set him an example of good conduct.

But to bear a sword, to do battle,
and to slaughter his enemies and their elephants,
that is the duty of this young man.

(Pu̱ranāṉūṟu - 312)

Episode 10

LAND IS GOOD ONLY WHEN MEN ARE GOOD

Sri Lanka (Ceylon) is a small country, but therein live two different nationalities with distinct languages, religions, cultures and geographical boundaries; one is called the Tamil Nation and the other the Sinhala Nation. The fact that the Sinhala government has been covertly and overtly engaged in the sinister and clandestine exercise of obliterating the boundaries between the two nations through deforestation and Sinhala colonisation does not mean that the boundaries have crumbled or that the nationalities have merged and integrated or that the right to self determination of the Tamils has disappeared.

Whenever an Eelam Tamil speaks of the struggle for liberation in Sri Lanka, arm-chair critics of the West and the East are inexplicably eager to mediate between the two warring nationalities and to proffer gratuitous advice. With apparent sympathy they pose the often plied question – “Is Tamil Eelam viable having regard to the smallness of the Eelam area and the hostile and infertile climate Eelam is said to have?” If Mauritius can be a separate entity, if Singapore can be an ideal country, if Maldives can be a peaceful country, why not Tamil Eelam, whose land area is much greater than that of those small countries? One can understand the crocodile tears which the cowardly critics shed. We all know too well the Tamil proverb "The wolf wailed that the lamb was getting drenched in the rain."

When I reflected upon the unsympathetic attitude of some of the Western countries that are fond of dismissing the Tamil's struggle for liberation in Sri Lanka as an impossible and puerile aspiration on the ground that another smaller nation within an already smallish nation would not be viable, I was reminded of a verse by the great Avvaiyār in the Pu̱ranāṉūṟu (Anthology of 400 war poems) dating back to the pre-Christian era.

In a way, this verse is the answer to the silly question which is time and time again raised by some of the international political pundits. Most of them are weather-cocks firmly entrenched in ivory towers and are minded to support only those that are strong and powerful. Unfortunately in this topsy-turvy world, they are the opinion makers! This is that verse in translation.

Oh land, dear land!
you may have fertile soil,
you may have wilderness,
you may have hollow valleys and high hills.
None of that matters:
only when the men you raise are good,
can you be called a good land!

(Puṟanāṉūṟu -187)

Tamils are good people. They want to live and let live. Therefore, the small size of Tamil Eelam is immaterial. The Jews of Jerusalem have proved the verse true and the Eelam Tamils will prove it too. If winter comes can spring be far behind?

Episode 11

PLEASE GO BACK

It was a difficult decision to take. To be ungrateful and insensitive to the feelings of their parents was unthinkable. To abandon overnight those two great souls that gave them succour and sustenance, hope and confidence, could be the greatest betrayal of faith one could think of. But the god-given bond of love that sprang up magnetically within a short spell of time was such that the boy and the girl, after some hesitation, introspection and retrospection, were emboldened to defy the wishes of their parents. They at last defied their parents, whom they had deified up to the moment of their hard resolve.

They decided to part company with their parents and eloped together. They set out on a long journey to a far off place which they thought their parents would not be able to discover, at least until they had got married properly and started new life as husband and wife. But they were nearly proved wrong, for less than two days after the would-be-couple escaped from their homesteads, the parents sent the girl's āyāh (nurse) to trace their whereabouts.

On the way the āyāh saw a group of holy men coming from the opposite direction. The sun was scorching, and to ward off the heat they were holding an umbrella. Urged by the desire to realise God, they appeared to be people going on a pilgrimage. Upon approaching the holymen, the āyāh enquired of them whether, by any chance, they saw on the way a girl and a boy who had, out of great love for each other, decided to become husband and wife much against the wishes of their parents.

As the āyāh was eagerly waiting for a response, one of the holymen opened his mouth to say "We were not unaware of them; we saw a boy who was the embodiment of all masculine virtues and a courageous and a beautifully bedecked girl of great nobility on the way. It would appear that you are the mother of that accomplished girl. You can now return home peacefully casting away your anxieties. You may ask why. Let me tell you.

The sweet smelling sandalwood grows on the hills. What use does the hill derive from that fragrant wood? It is those who smear the sandal paste on their body who derive benefit from sandal.

The much-sought-after and valued pearls are produced in the sea and what use are they to the sea? It is the people who wear them who enjoy those pearls.

The sweet music of the lute originates from the strings of the lute. But do the strings get any benefit or pleasure from such music? No. This exactly is the situation with your daughter also.

Your daughter is a girl of surpassing chastity and virtue. She can withstand the strain of this world through her virtuous qualities. She has chosen the best partner for her life. What she has done is the right thing. Do not lament that your daughter has taken the course she has taken. Please go home with peace of mind".

This drama is contained in a Kalittokai poem of twenty four lines. Here is the English rendering.

The āyāh says:

Oh you holy men who walk under the shadow of your parasols,
to protect you from the burning sun,
with cord-slung pitchers and triple staves
carefully balanced on your shoulders;
your minds are focused and your senses all controlled;
and you tread this earth out of a sense of duty.
On your way here, did you good men happen to see
my daughter with another woman's son?
They both knew full well what they were doing
and now are joined together as one.

The holy men reply:

We did indeed see them on our way here,
we could not miss them.
So you are the mother of the well dressed girl,
who dared to set out with that handsome boy
along the rough jungle path?
Please listen and reflect.

The fragrant sandal paste is no use to the mountain
from which it comes;
it is only of use to those who apply it to their skin.
When you come to think about it,
it is the same with your daughter.
Again the rare, lustrous pearl is no use to the water
in which it was produced,
but only to those who wear it.
When you stop to consider,
it is the same with your daughter.
Similarly, sweet music is no use to the lute
on which it is played,
but only to the player.
When you reflect,
it is the same with your daughter.
There is no point in lamenting the loss of your daughter;
there is no better man that she could have gone off with.
The best course now is for her to stay with him.

(Kalittokai-08)

Episode 12

I SHED MY SHYNESS

Tamil literature traditionally classifies love into three categories: (a) The love that subsists between a boy and a girl who are equal in their appearance, wealth, character and social status; (b) The love which is one sided, that is where one party loves the other, while the other does not; and (c) The love that is shown between people who should not be life partners; for example, between an old man and a young girl. Tamils refer to the first category as "Aṉpiṉ Aintiṇai"; the second as "Kaikkiḷai"; and the third as "Peruntiṇai" or "Poruntākkāmam".

Tamil literature has accorded a status to "Kaikkiḷai" (one-sided love or unilateral love); but has not accorded any status to "Peruntiṇai" or "Poruntākkāmam" as the poets were of the firm conviction that such "love" (lust) between unfit partners should not be tolerated or accepted in a decent society. Let us now see how Kaikkiḷai is depicted in a poem from the Kalittokai anthology.

The father of the girl was a landed proprietor who owned acres of arable land where he cultivated cereals such as green gram, black gram, millet and maize. To prevent the crops from being destroyed by birds like parrots and doves, the girl, along with other family members, used to take turns and keep watch at the plantation from wooden watchtowers constructed out of bamboo. To minimize the tedium and to while away the time, small swings were also constructed on which the girls who kept guard could amuse themselves.

One day when the girl was at her father's farm, there came running a boy carrying a bow and arrow. He appeared to be looking for his quarry which he had wounded with an arrow. He was sporting on his head a floral ornament. Upon seeing the girl, he stood there and looked at her for a while. But he did not speak a word, though his face betrayed that he was enamoured by the beauty of the girl. The same thing happened on many subsequent occasions. His actions perplexed the girl and she began to pity him, feeling innocently for him. Her sympathy for that boy was such that she almost became preoccupied with thoughts of him. These thoughts cut short her sleep and raised concerns in her. She wished that he should speak up and disclose his feelings. But he would not. As for her, her modesty prevented her from initiating any conversation. This was her predicament. She feared that he might commit suicide. She began to pine and as a consequence started to lose weight. This was a sign that she had developed a liking for the boy. Her physical weakness gave her mental boldness.

One day while she was playing on the swing, this boy approached again and stood still a few yards away from her as had become his custom. The girl mustered courage and asked him, "Could you please push this swing, sir." He obliged and pushed the swing so that she swung to and fro. Snatching the opportunity, she feigned unconsciousness, let go of the rope gradually and "fell" backwards onto his broad chest. Believing that she had in fact become unconscious, he lifted her off the swing and held her securely in his arms. Relishing the grip of the boy, the girl stayed in that position, fearing that if she were to open her eyes, he would set her on the ground and bid her a safe journey home. Such a chivalrous boy he was!

In the poem given below the girl narrates her experience to her girl friend.

Listen to me, my dark-eyed friend!
Some time ago, a young man used to come by
with a bow and arrows in his hand,
and flowers in his hair.
Supposedly, he had shot and hit his quarry,
and was now in hot pursuit of it.
He would look at me in a way that showed he fancied me,
but he never said a word outright.
My heart was not drawn to him,
but still I could not sleep at night
for the pity that I felt at his distress.
He hesitated to speak his mind,

and I too coyly held my peace.
Some time passed, and then
I did something quite unseemly for a woman.
Just listen to this, my friend with the lovely scent!
One day we went to the farm
where we used to scare off the parrots from the crops.
There I was sitting on the swing
when this young man came past,
still looking at me in the same way as he did before.
I shook off my former modesty, and said,
"Please will you give me a push!"
"Certainly", he said, and I swung to and fro.
Then, pretending to faint, I lost my hold on the rope
and fell backwards into his arms.
He held me firmly,
as I lay content in his embrace.
If I came round too soon,
I was afraid that he would send me home.
So I pretended that I was still unconscious.
He was such a gentleman!

(Kuriñcikkali -01)

Episode 13

A DARING DISPLAY OF LOVE

The love poems of the Caṅkam age have as their themes the natural ups and downs on the rough route of lovers, from the time they set eyes on each other until they get married and settle happily in life, or separate from each other after marriage for one reason or another. Normally the episodes painted in the poems are love at first sight. The lover and the beloved thereafter meet at a secret rendezvous. Somehow the meetings rouse the suspicion of the neighbours. Fearing that the parents will not agree to their marriage, the girl elopes with the boy and starts a settled married life. They are no more the lover and the beloved. They are now husband and wife.

Married life imposes many responsibilities and the husband goes away to far off places in search of wealth, or goes to the battlefield to defend his country at the behest of his king. This results in the wife not being able to see her husband for months. The painful and impatient waiting of the wife for the return of the husband and the impatience of the husband to rejoin his wife are discussed beautifully in the love poems of the Caṅkam age. The Kāmattuppāl of the Tirukkuṟaḷ is an exemplary poetic painting of this gradual process of courtship and of the concomitant pain and pleasure of the metamorphosis of that exciting period into a settled married life.

There is an interesting poem in Kalittokai which brilliantly portrays how a girl who was not sure whether she really loved a boy or not is ultimately wooed by the boy in an artistically deceptive manner. This incident is painted by the great poet Kapilar in a story form. The lovelorn girl narrates to her companion how her boyfriend accomplished his mission.

"One day my mother and I were at home. All the others were out. We heard a shout from outside, begging for some water to drink. Hearing this, my mother said 'Dear daughter! Someone at the door wants some water to quench their thirst. Please take some water in the golden jar for them to drink.' Without wasting any time I filled the golden jar with water and hurried to the door to pour it for the caller to drink. My dear friend! Guess what I saw there? Do you remember that miscreant who, a couple of days ago, came to us, when we were building houses of sand by the roadside, and trampled upon them with his feet? I mean that very smart fellow who had the temerity to pull out the flowers which we were wearing on our hair and make us cry. That very mischievous fellow who picked up the ball we were playing with and disappeared with it?

It was he who was standing there. It was a shock to me but I tried to conceal my surprise. I extended the jar of water to him. Instead of taking the jar from me he grasped my wrist passionately. I gave a sudden cry uttering 'Oh mother! Come and see what he has done.' Hearing my cry and realising that something untoward happened, my mother came rushing to the door.

I did not know what to tell my mother. I pitied the fellow. Perhaps I loved him in my heart of hearts! So I did not have the heart to betray him. I thought out a ruse then and there, and told mother that while drinking the water he choked and was short of breath. My mother unquestioningly believed what I said, and sat him on her lap and started stroking his back to relieve his assumed pain caused by the hiccup. As my mother was doing this in all good faith, the mischievous fellow stole a killing look at me through the corner of his eye evoking sensual passions in me."

Let us now see the English version of this Kalittokai poem which is a poor substitute for the original in the Tamil Language.

Listen to my story, my friend with the glittering bangles.
My mother and I were all alone in the house
when we heard a call from outside:
"Hello there! Please would you give me a drink of water
to quench my thirst"
My mother told me to take him some water in the golden pot.
So when, in all innocence, I took the water to the door,
I was shocked to see who it was that had called.
It was the same troublesome young fellow
who used to follow us around and tease us.

When we built sand castles by the road side,
he would trample all over them.
He would pull out the flowers we wore in our hair,
and run off with our ball.
When I recognised him, I hid my surprise,
but as I held out the water to him
suddenly he grasped my bangled wrist.
"Mother, look what he is doing!" I cried.
But when my mother came running out
and asked me what the matter was,
I told her,
"The water went down the wrong way as he drank
and he choked on it."
At once my mother patted him gently on the back.
And all the while with a furtive grin
he shot glances at me out of the corner of his eye,
the rascal!

(Kalittokai – 51)

Episode 14

THE PENCIL AND THE EYEBROW

Poetry has three important elements, namely feeling, imagination and beautiful sound effect. We could compare poetry to a lady; feeling is the soul of the poetry lady; imagination is her body and the sound effect is her dress. Imagination and the sound effect are there to sustain the soul of poetry which is the feeling. Poetry can exist without beautiful sound effects but a composition will cease to be poetry if it is bereft of feelings or imagination. Although they may be found to be exaggerated, they will not be totally untrue.

The very fact that poetry is a combination of feelings and imagination would mean that poetry cannot be experienced or enjoyed unless one is prepared to transform oneself into a child and to live in a world of dreams. If one were to enjoy a dream, one should not, at the same time, try to live in the real world; not only that; one should not even think that one is dreaming. The moment your brain wakes up and realises that what you are seeing is a dream, the dream will disappear.

Anyone who wants to enjoy poetry must employ the immature and tender brain of a child, forget the real world and enter the dream world. Though it is true with any poetry, it is even more so with Tamil poetry. It is then that you could enter the dream world of the child. It is in that world one could enjoy poetry fully. Those that want to play and relax in the world of imagination must be prepared to shed a lot of their experiences and knowledge and get into a state of semi-ignorance. Just as people who wish to play with infants must put aside their mature knowledge and transform themselves into innocent babes, those that want to float hilariously in the world of imagination should, at least to a certain extent, abandon their faculty of discretion.

With this introduction let us see a love scene painted by Tiruvaḷḷuvar.

A girl started a love affair with a boy with the connivance of her worldly wise foster-mother (chaperon). They began to like each other, and met at intervals at pre-arranged venues and times, with the cooperation of the foster-mother, but without the knowledge of their natural parents. On one occasion it so happened that the boy could not keep his appointment. The girl was thoroughly upset and confused. She was so furious that she complained harshly to her foster-mother. Realising the frustration of the girl caused by the boy's failure to turn up as scheduled, the foster-mother tried to console the girl giving plausible explanations on the boy's behalf. The anguish of the girl was such that she did not seem to be comforted. The girl went on recalling previous incidents where the boy had behaved in the same way. She swore that she would not set eyes on him again. She said that her anger would not cool until she had repaid him in the same coin. Fearing that any further cajoling or comforting could harden the girl's resolve, the foster-mother kept quiet and diffused the situation for the time being.

A few days passed and the lovelorn girl received a secret message from the boy asking her to meet him at a designated place and time. The very receipt of the message from the boy sent electric impulses through her body. She felt ecstatic. Even so, in the presence of the foster-mother she pretended that the message from the boy had no effect on her. Days moved very slowly. Eventually the day came and the very minute neared, and the girl's heart was signalling her brain to rush to the rendezvous. However the girl pretended to be indifferent and otherwise engaged. The foster-mother feared that the girl's pledge to pay the boy in the same coin could lead to complications; so she hurried to the girl's apartment and politely reminded her of the appointment. The girl put on a practised sulking face and proceeded reluctantly with the foster-mother to the meeting point, where the boy was impatiently waiting with a heart full of pent-up emotions and feelings.

No sooner had the eyes of the lovers met than all her pretensions and modesty melted away and her face bloomed radiantly. The foster-mother, who was there with trepidation fearing that something untoward could happen, was taken aback. She could not believe her eyes. She breathed a sigh of relief. Realising that her continued presence could dampen the pleasure of the young lovers, she slipped away.

The girl, after giving full vent to her stored up passions and feelings surreptitiously returned to her apartment. The foster-mother was a sagacious and well-meaning but at times mischievous woman. She followed the girl into her apartment chuckling. The meaning of the chuckle was obvious. Even so, the girl asked why she was chuckling so mischievously. The foster-mother replied:

"The behaviour of love-stricken girls is beyond comprehension. It was only the other day you were calling that boy names and swearing at him. But when you met him today you did not even ask him why he disappointed you last time. Instead you simply ran to him and embraced him. Is that all your resolution amounts to?"

The girl blushed and tried to bluff; she remembered a Kuṟaḷ which she had learnt a couple of weeks ago, and which she thought would extricate her from her predicament. She picked up her eyebrow pencil and said:

"My dear mother, please listen. Look at this pencil. You and I use this pencil to paint our eyebrows every day. Don't we? We are able to see this pencil clearly now; but the moment we pick it up and put it close to our eyebrow, we cease to see it. Why is that? We don't see the pencil because our concentration is focused elsewhere. When we begin to paint, our concentration is on the eyebrow and not on the pencil. Similarly when my boyfriend is away from me, I see his lapses and faults magnified and large. But when he is close to me, just as we cease to see the pencil when it is near our eyebrow, I forget his faults and lapses. Such is the nature of my love. When I am close to him I don't see any of his faults, but when I am away from him, I see nothing but his faults."

The foster mother was non-plussed, but admired the presence of mind of the girl. The lesson which the above Kuṟaḷ teaches is that the mistakes of those that are far from us are glaringly obvious. But the mistakes of those that are close by are not visible to our eyes, mental or physical. That is human nature. We must guard ourselves against selfishness which makes us blind and prevents us from seeing the truth. Now read the translation of the Kuṟaḷ.

Just as the eye cannot see the pencil
as it paints the eyebrow,
So when I am close to him,
I cannot see my lover's faults.

(Tirukkuṟaḷ - 1285)

Episode 15

A FEELING OF SHEER HELPLESSNESS

It might well be that certain poems in the Tamil classical literature would sound irrelevant to the time we are living in, particularly when we think of the foreign culture in which we have been placed. Perhaps it may be irrelevant also in the context of present day Tamil Eelam or South India. But the reader should bear in mind that these poems are two thousand years old and were born in a situation when it was the literary fashion to depict the woman as the passive partner in an episode of courtship. With this prelude let us see yet another painting in a Kuṟuntokai poem.

She was an innocent girl. She fell for the boy and she passionately longed to have him as her life partner. He promised to marry her. But his duty for the nation demanded his going to the battlefield, and he went promising the girl that he would be back by a certain date. Time moved slowly and the appointed date passed, but he did not show up. Enquiries made of him did not yield the response she wished to hear. She could not believe that he could disappoint her, nor could she be certain that he would honour his promise. Her thoughts ran riot. She started thinking of the times he had spent with her at their secret rendezvous cuddling and fondling. The fear "what shall I do if he fails to honour his promise to marry me" gripped her, and her insecure feelings made her thoughts wander and think the unthinkable. "How could I prove that he in fact promised to marry me", she asked herself.

The thought that no other human was present when he cuddled her and made the promise tormented her. In her helplessness, as a last resort she began to comfort herself by saying "yes there was no other human being present except the thief himself when he made the promise. But there was a stork which was looking patiently for fish in the running water. At least that will bear testimony to the fact that my lover promised to marry me even though he now appears to have deserted me". Here is the English rendering of that beautiful poem which is in the form of a soliloquy.

There was no one present to witness
the promise that he made to me
on that fateful day.
Only a solitary stork stood still in the shallow water
with thin greenish legs like stalks of millet,
fishing for sprats.
If he breaks his promise and cheats on me,
what on earth can I do?

(Kuṟuntokai -25)

Episode 16

AN INEXPLICABLE BOND

Love is a wonderful thing. At the same time it is something difficult to define. All religionists say that the bond of love between an individual soul and the Supreme Being is its highest form, and the love that subsists between a man and a woman, or between husband and wife is inferior to the spiritual bond between a human being and the Almighty. That is why the Tamils refer to the love between man and God as *pēriṉpam* (supreme bliss) and the one that exists between man and woman as *ciṟṟiṉpam* (lesser bliss). In an attempt to define love which he calls Kāmam in the Tirukkuṟaḷ, Tiruvaḷḷuvar says that love is finer than a flower and that only very few understand it.

The love that comes into being all of a sudden and overnight between a husband and his wife defies explanation. To say that such a bond of love results from sexual desire is to over-simplify matters. There is something more than that sexual attraction, which the scientists and the psychologists have failed to explain. It is because of this, at least in Tamil societies, there results a hatred for the daughter-in-law on the part of the parents of the husband. The son who was so dear to them and who loved them to the core of his being until the moment of his marriage, overnight transfers all his love and affection to a new woman who knows next to nothing about the boy. The parents of the husband not only hate their daughter-in-law but also criticise their son, saying that he is behaving like a puppet moving his hands and feet at the beck and call of the new person who has now become his wife.

This feature in the life of a new couple must have surprised our ancient poets also. In a Kuṟuntokai poem a poet called Cempulap Peyal Nīrār has expressed his surprise at the inexplicable feeling of love which a husband shows towards his wife and vice versa. The poem takes the form of an interjection on the part of the boy-husband. He says: "Your mother is not at all known to my mother; likewise your father and my father are not related to each other. Until the day of our marriage there was no occasion for you to know me or for me to learn of you. The elders brought us together and said that we are now partners and we will be partners forever. That is all; and our heart and soul have merged together inseparably, like pure water that falls on red clay soil and assumes the colour of the soil. How has this happened! Is it not the work of God? Now have a look at the translation of that Tamil poem.

What has your mother to do with mine?
Or what relation is my father to yours?
So how did you and I ever get to know each other?
But just as the rain water
takes on the colour of the soil on which it falls,

so when we fell in love,

our hearts became inseparable.

(Kuṟuntokai -40)

Episode 17

THE POWER OF LOVE

This is another wonderful scene from Kuṟuntokai revealing one of the mysteries of nature and the Almighty. Whatever modern thinkers and feminists might say, the capacity for patience and selflessness is God's gift to the female species only. It is equally true in the jungle also. Humans are bent on avoiding pain and desiring pleasure. Even so, even an uneducated and immature young girl inexplicably assumes the role of a mature woman, the moment she crosses the threshold of married life. How does this happen?

If we look back on our own youthful days, we will remember vividly many occasions when we adamantly refused to eat the food prepared by our mother, making complaints about its quality. We have rejected food which was prepared by our mother with the utmost care and consideration for our well being. This is not peculiar to male or female. It is common to both sexes. But the moment he or she gets married, there occurs a sudden change in the attitude of the person. The selfishness that dominated his pre-marriage life gives way to a kind of selflessness or altruism. This phenomenon is well captured in a Kuṟuntokai poem as follows.

There lived a girl and a boy who loved each other passionately. They wanted to get married, but the parents of the girl thought that she could be given in marriage to a boy of their choice who was better off than the boy their daughter had given her heart to. This resulted in the girl eloping with her lover and establishing a new household. The parents of the girl learnt of it, but refused to patch up their quarrel with the young couple. Days and weeks passed, running into months. The resolve of the girl's mother began to melt and relent, and she sent the woman who was the āyāh (nurse) of the girl to her daughter's house to see whether she was doing all right. The mother asked the āyāh not to mention to her daughter that she had gone there only at the request of the mother.

The āyāh, who had reluctantly refrained all these months from going to the house of the new couple, was delighted beyond measure, and she set out to see her step-daughter who was living miles away from her. When she reached the house of the couple, she was stunned with delight by what she saw there in the kitchen. She was so pleased at the sight that she stayed outside the mud house and watched what was happening inside. The girl was busy cooking.

The āyāh quietly got closer to the kitchen wall to see what curries or dishes she was preparing. She was in the process of preparing yoghurt gravy *tayirkkuḻampu*. The young wife took out a tumbler of curd and started crushing it with her beautiful fingers resembling the flower petals of Kāntaḷ (*Gloriosa superba*). She then put the requisite spices and seasoning in the frying pan. As the pan of curry was simmering, she felt the saree on her waist slowly slipping. She feared that if she rinsed her fingers before adjusting the saree, the preparation on the fire might become over-cooked and lose its flavour. So she adjusted the saree with her fingers still covered with curd.

As the condiments in the frying pan started to sizzle, a cloud of smoke rose from the pan and went into her eyes that were closely watching the pan to assess the state of cooking. The smoke that went direct into her eyes made her eyes water, thus impairing her vision and causing irritation in the eyes. Unmindful of all this pain and discomfort, she wiped her eyes with the tip of the saree head piece and continued her cooking to ensure a tasty preparation. Realising that the food should be eaten hot, she softly called *Attāṉ*. Her man came smiling and sat on the floor to eat the food his beloved had prepared for him. No sooner had she served some rice and curry on the banana leaf plate than he said "wonderful", "brilliant", "very tasty". Upon hearing these words from her husband, she blushed and her face beamed with happiness. This is the scene painted in verse number 167 of the Kuṟuntokai.

The life of this girl before she started to live with her husband was different, totally different. She was always, like any girl, conscious of herself. She spent hours and hours polishing her nails and applying cutex. She hated the idea of chopping chillies or peeling onions for fear that such work would spoil the beauty of her slender fingers and nails. She avoided exposing her eyes to heat or smoke lest the beauty of her eyes should be destroyed by perspiration. She was so fastidious that she changed her clothes frequently to ensure that they looked spotless. Such was her concern about her nails, eyes, fingers and dress before marriage.

After her marriage, her concern for herself disappeared in a jiffy and she ceased to be self-centred. After marriage all that she longed for was the happiness of her partner. That is why she could spend hours and hours in the kitchen preparing nice dishes for her husband at the expense of the once carefully maintained beauty of her nails, fingers, eyes and clothes.

In the case of the boy also the situation was similar. Before marriage he was so selfish and it was his likes and dislikes that mattered most. This being so, even the best of dishes prepared for him by his mother did not taste good and he did not speak well of them. His selfishness prevented him from realising the truth when he was living in the house of his mother. However when he got married and surrendered himself to his partner, his selfishness dissolved and the girl's preparations tasted like ambrosia because of his change of heart and attitude to life.

Let us now see the Tamil verse in translation.

After kneading the thick yoghurt,
she wiped her hands on her saree.
In her anxiety to finish cooking the meal
before her husband came home,
she had no time to change her clothes or rinse her fingers.
As she hurriedly prepared the sweet and sour curry,
the steam got in her eyes and made them run.
Unmindful of the discomfort
she called her husband.
But when he sat down to eat
and obviously enjoyed his meal,
her face beamed with pleasure.

(Kuṟuntokai -167)

Episode 18

TWO COCKS ON THE DUNG HEAP

The love torn girl could not hide her love for long. Somehow her parents got to know that she was in love with a boy. They prevented her from going out except under supervision. Confined to the house most of the time, the girl was hoping that her boyfriend would, without loss of time, make arrangements to marry her. But the boy, because of his problems with his parents, could not do what his girl friend hoped for. This increased her worry and fear. She grew more and more hopeless and suffered within herself unable to speak out her misery. When her maid approached to console her, she gave vent to her pent up feelings of love and disappointment by comparing her mental state to that of the free-range fighting cocks at the dung heap at the back of her house which she had enjoyed watching when she was young. She spoke thus:

"The flame of passionate love which was brought upon me by my eyes saps my health to the core of my bones; but I am not able to join him to embrace him. My friend is also not able to reach me to get rid of my misery. My position is like a fight between two free-range cocks at the dung heap, which are wont to fight to the death as there is nobody to separate them." The comparison here is remarkable. It is only poets of the highest order with a keen power of observation of nature who could aptly make such appropriate comparisons.

Way back in Sri Lanka, and Tamil Nadu many readers will have enjoyed watching cock fights, which are natural and routine events there. However in India, there are professional people who rear fighting cocks so that, through making them fight with cocks owned by similar professionals, they are able to make a living.

There is a marked difference between the natural fight of the free range cocks and the artificially incited fight of commercially raised cocks. In the case of commercial cock fights, the cocks themselves have no right either to start their fight with the other cock or to stop from fighting. It is the owner of the cock who will decide when the cock should start the fighting and when it should stop. The owner of a winning cock has the power to allow his cock to fight until the other cock is defeated or immobilised or to stop it halfway through. The owner of the cock which is defeated completely, or is about to be defeated, will also have the right to withdraw his cock and stop the fight. In other words, in the case of commercial cock fighting, there is somebody to stop the fight. The situation is different in the case of free range cocks that fight at the dung-heap on their own accord, without the involvement or intervention of a human third party. It is the cocks that start the fight on the dung heap, and there is no one to start the fight or to put an end to it. Consequently the dung-heap-cocks go on fighting until one of them wins the fight or gets defeated or even killed.

The composer of this poem in Kuṟuntokai whose birth name is not known, was a nature poet like Wordsworth of England. When the poet had occasion to watch one of the free range cock fights on the roadside near a dung heap, he was reminded of the mental pangs of the love-torn girl we have seen above. Because her affair with the boy friend is hidden from her parents and friends, there is nobody to intervene to relieve her of her misery. Consequently her misery continues unabated like the misery of the free range cocks which have no one to intervene to relieve them of the pain of fighting. Now this is the English translation of that Kuṟuntokai poem.

It was through my eyes
that this burning love was kindled within me.
Now although it has penetrated to the marrow of my bones,
still I cannot reach out and hold him in my arms.
Neither can he come close
to relieve my misery.
Like a pair of cocks fighting on the dung heap,
I am in a fight to the death
with the sickness that assails me.
And there is no one who can rid me of it.

(Kuṟuntokai -305)

Episode 19
THE PAIN REVEALING PLEASURE

Neruñci is the name of a thorny shrub with beautiful yellow blooms. It is a tropical plant with a partiality for dry soil. It is a common sight in the sun scorched soil of Jaffna, Sri Lanka. There could be few Tamils who have not seen it, nor felt the piercing pain of being pricked by its thorny fruits. Many of us know how beautiful its tiny flowers are and how those flowers transform into roundish balls of spikes upon maturation. However *neruñci* never appears to be of any significance to many of us. It is here that we differ from the way poets look at things.

The blind do not realise the beauty of a gold bangle. The sweetness of good music cannot be appreciated by a deaf person. Likewise the wonderful greatness of nature is not realised by people who are not endowed with a heart that feels. Poets are out of the ordinary people who are capable of apprehending the actual facts of physical things, and appreciating and admiring the nature of the feelings that throb in the heart of nature.

Poets are endowed with wings of imagination. They are said to be possessed of very sharp and penetrating mental eyes capable of x-raying life's realities. It is in this respect that poets differ from ordinary people like us. This is evidenced in many poems of the Caṅkam period, notably the Kuṟuntokai. There is a poem in the Kuṟuntokai where the author uses *neruñci* as an analogy to illustrate a point. The author of the poem is Naṉmullaiyār.

In the village where Naṉmullaiyār lived, there lived a couple who were lawfully married. At the beginning they were a happy couple. As time passed the husband developed an interest in another woman and became unfaithful to his wedded wife. His infatuation for the new woman was such that at times he stayed away at night with the other woman. His guilty conscience prevented him from being free and open to his wedded wife. He became estranged from his wife and less cordial towards her. His wife was worried and puzzled. She tried to find out the reason for the sudden change in the feelings and behaviour of her husband. He bluffed and blustered and pretended that nothing had gone wrong. But the prolonged indifference of her husband pained her a lot and she pined for him. There was no change of heart in sight.

Poet Naṉmullaiyār, who heard of the pangs of near-separation of this couple whom he had known from the time they were married, thought of the days when the couple were honeymooning and feeling on top of the world, and compared their initial rollicking days with the present predicament of the girl.

When he thought of the plight of the pitiful girl, he was reminded of the different phases in the life history of the *neruñci* shrub, and his imagination took wings to produce a beautiful love poem. Naṉmullaiyār has composed the poem assuming himself to be the forsaken wife. The poet's imagination runs thus:

The yellow *neruñci* flowers are pleasing to the eyes at the beginning. They remain so for some time. As time passes the yellow petals fall one by one and then the petal-less flower develops small spines which gradually transform into prickly and pain-inflicting thorns. This is how my husband has also become. During the days that preceded and followed the honey-moon, my husband was pleasing to see and sweet to touch. Of late, like the beautiful *neruñci* flower which becomes a sharp thorn later, my once loving husband has become a source of pain and menace. Let us now see the translation of the Tamil poem.

I am sick at heart, really sick at heart!
At first the cow-thorn with its dainty leaves
puts out fresh flowers;
but later on, its sharp thorns grow.
So at first my lover was all kindness,
but he has now turned nasty,
and I am sick at heart.

(Kuṟuntokai -202)

Episode 20

WHEN EVEN A PIG IS VIGILANT

There is no country in the world which is free from superstitions. English people have some superstitious beliefs about Friday and the number thirteen. They also believe that seven is a lucky number. English people speak of "lucky seven" and "sweet sixteen". It is this superstitious belief which has given rise to the pseudo science called numerology.

Tamils have a belief that the cawing of a crow in the morning perched on a tree in the compound of their house is a sign that they should expect some unexpected visitor on that day. There is a superstition among the Tamils that if the long tailed sparrow hops around on the tree top or the roof of a house and wails, then there will occur an unexpected death in the family. Tamils harbour a belief that it would be dangerous for them to continue their journey if they chance to see a cat crossing the path as they step out of their house. Tamil literature makes us believe that it is an ill omen if the right eye of a woman twinkles and twitches, and that a twinkle or twitch in the left eye is good omen.

Tamils of Sri Lanka have a notion that a person will come upon good fortune and wealth if he or she experiences an itchy feeling in the palm of their hand. English people also appear to entertain a similar belief.

Tamils all over the world believe that wall lizards are their friends and that they are endowed with the faculty of predicting future events. Tamil literature tells us that the ancient Tamils attached some importance to the chirping of wall lizards. There is a poem in Naṟṟiṇai from which we learn that the Tamils of yore, as of today, willy-nilly believed that there was something to gain by listening to the chirping of wall lizards which are called *palli* in the Tamil language. Let us now see the contextual setting of the Naṟṟiṇai poem under consideration.

There was a boy who was in love with a girl. The boy was honest and genuine. He loved the girl passionately and continued to visit her at a secret rendezvous at night. She was the daughter of a petty feudal lord whose palatial building was strongly guarded. His meeting her at night was always fraught with danger in that if by any chance the palace guards caught him they would harm him or lock him up. This very thought tormented her. The fear that he might be exposed to other dangers as well on the roads during the night also concerned her. So she decided to tell him that he should no longer continue this kind of dating and that he should make immediate arrangements to marry her. But she felt that it would be rude on her part to say that to her lover in so many words and so she conveyed her intention in a round about way. This is how she conveyed her feelings:

"You are the proud lord of a resourceful mountainous country in whose jungles wild boars roam. I have heard of many blood curdling incidents that took place in these jungles. Let me narrate one such incident. Please listen seriously. One day a wild boar grew hungry and decided to go to a vegetable farm to fill its stomach. With a view to warding off animals and birds which destroy their crops, the owners of the farm had set up traps at vantage points to ensnare such destructive animals and birds. This wild boar went to the usual entrance of the farm and found the entrance strewn with traps. It was nothing new to it. On earlier occasions it had managed to gain entry without getting trapped. It was confident that it could do that again successfully this time also.

So, after sizing up the situation, it moved towards the trap. Just then it heard the chirping of a wall lizard which was perched on a rock nearby. The chirping of the lizard made the boar think. Never before had this happened to it. Being abnormally intelligent, it thought that the chirping of the lizard was the warning of a danger lying ahead. Without further ado, the boar retraced its steps and retired to its hideout. You are the proud owner of the jungles where such intelligent animals live. Because you daily come to see me every night on dangerous roads exposing yourself to all manner of risks, I am not able to get a wink of sleep. My eyes are always on the look out for you, and they get no rest."

By implication she tried to tell him that when animals themselves are able to sense danger and avoid it, it is utterly irresponsible if as a human being he failed to realise all the dangers ahead of him. In other words she tried to tell him that he should refrain from the dangerous practice of courting in this way, and that severe vigilance on the part of the palace guards could result in his being prevented from meeting her at all, as had happened to the wild boar. He should therefore put an end to his visits and resort to the direct route of marrying her without further delay. Let us now see the English rendition of the poem.

A stray pig covered in bristles
approached the farm in search of food.
On a rock by the path the farmer had set a snare;
but undeterred the pig pressed on.
Then as it neared the rock, it heard a lizard chirping in a crevice.
Taking that as a warning of some danger,
the intelligent animal at once took fright,
and fled back to its lair.
There are a lot of pigs like that round here!
Although by night my house is closely guarded,
you still dare to come waiting for the moment
when the watchman's attention wanders.
What is worse, I cannot sleep for fear of the risks you run.

(*Naṟṟiṇai – 98*)

Episode 21

A YOUNG WIFE OF GREAT MATURITY

Naṟṟiṇai Nāṉūṟu also called Naṟṟiṇai is an anthology of classical poems. It is included in the larger anthology called "Eṭṭuttokai" which itself contains eight smaller anthologies of which Naṟṟiṇai is one. Let us look at another painting contained in a Naṟṟiṇai poem.

The poem is about a girl who has learnt the art of living, having gone through thick and thin. She married the boy whom she loved, and moved to the house of her husband to set up a separate home. She was no ordinary girl; she was born in the lap of luxury. Her parents were well to do and she was the apple of their eyes. She knew no worries when she was with her parents. She had servants and others to attend to her needs. Her husband was a nice boy and the honeymoon was fine.

As time passed her husband fell on hard days and their financial condition began to deteriorate, forced them to forgo even necessaries and to miss meals. Even a square meal proved to be a luxury. Her husband was pained to see the obvious misery his wife was enduring. But the girl was happy to undergo the pain together with her husband. She performed her wifely duties unflinchingly without complaint. She would not allow herself to think of the luxurious life she had lived when she was with her parents.

One day her mother visited her daughter in her husband's home. The physical glow which her daughter had before marriage had faded; she looked pale and emaciated. But the mother saw her daughter beaming with joy; it was not a joy that was put on but natural and genuine. She watched her daughter perform her daily chores and routine duties for some time, and was amazed to see how frugally she was managing her household. While she felt sorry for the penury in which her daughter languished, she was pleased to see the commendable transformation in her. She had a flashback and was reminded of her daughter's youth when even feeding her was a Herculean task. Her thoughts ran thus:

"What a luxurious life my daughter lived when she was in her parents' home! What a poverty-stricken life she is leading now! When she was young she was fed luxurious food on gold plates, and the servant maids had to run after her with a soft cane to make her eat. Then, she would run out of the house and refuse to come back to have her next mouthful. Such was her behaviour when she was with us. She was so young that she did not learn even the basics of the culinary art. Despite her tender age she developed a fancy for a boy of her choice and reluctantly we gave her in marriage to him, though we knew that she was not yet fully ready for married life. She bade goodbye to us and left us to start a life of her own. As we knew her inadequacies and immaturity, we harboured the fear that she would not be able to cope with married life and that untoward things might happen.

Upon coming here to see her, I realise that we have been proved wrong. I am puzzled and at a loss to understand how my little daughter learnt the homely arts of neatness, frugality and house keeping as well as a sense of service to her husband. While looking after herself she has also learnt the art of keeping her husband contented by being faithful, dutiful and chaste. She does not long for the life she led when she was a child. She does not hate the hand-to-mouth existence she is now leading. She has developed the rare quality of contentment." All these thoughts coursed through her motherly mind in quick succession, and she felt happy and proud for her daughter.

The following poem from "Naṟṟiṇai Nāṉūṟu", a rough English translation of which is given below, contains the episode described above.

How did this girl become so clever?
When her husband fell on hard times,
she learned to cut her coat according to her cloth,
and refused the treats her father offered her.
As a young child she had been notoriously mischievous.

One day her old nurse brought her
honey and milk in a bright golden pot.
With a cane in her other hand,
the nurse told her to drink her milk.
But she ran off, darting to and fro,
to the tinkling of her pearl-studded anklets.
At last the nurse gave up,
frustrated by her antics.
How did such a girl become so responsible?

(Naṟṟiṇai- 110)

Episode 22

ECONOMIC JUSTICE ENVISAGED BY TIRUVAḺḺUVAR

A close study of the Tirukkuṟaḷ will reveal that human community was a dominant theme of Tiruvaḷḷuvar's treatise. This perhaps is the reason why he considered men of the earth to be superior to those said to be living in the heavens. It is this conviction that made him emphasise that he who lives righteously in this world will be treated on equal terms with those living in the heavens. He realised that for a person to live an honest and righteous life, the country he lives in must be a perfect country.

What is the meaning of a "perfect country"? Is there any definition of such a thing? Yes there is. Tiruvaḷḷuvar has given a definition. In fact he has given many equally good definitions, two of which are worth mentioning. One definition says that a perfect country is one which can look after itself without seeking assistance from outside; and a country which can survive only at the mercy of others cannot be said to be perfect. Sri Lanka is an example of such a country. Sri Lanka relies for its existence on India, Pakistan, China and Japan and the European Union. Realising that certain groups of people might not consider that to be an acceptable definition, Tiruvaḷḷuvar supplements the first definition with another, which is fuller and more comprehensive. He says that a perfect country is one which is free from persistent starvation, widespread diseases and never ending enemies. Sri Lanka is a negative candidate for this second definition also.

The word "enemies" needs elucidation. Enemies can be of two kinds, external enemy and internal enemy. External enemies can be tackled by the government with the help of armed forces such as the army, navy and air force. The internal enemy is difficult to define. It is a conglomeration of many forces. There are many reasons for the existence of this internal enemy and it assumes many forms. The cause for the internal enemy is the disparity and imbalance in the society, which gives rise to quarrels, disaffection, dissatisfaction and disorder. Superstitions and social disabilities such as casteism also create internal enemies.

It is the responsibility of the government to ensure that social disabilities and communal disparities are eradicated from the society. A society riddled with diseases cannot think of development or prosperity. Therefore it is the paramount duty of the government to ensure that the country is disease-free.

The third *sine qua non* for an ideal country is the absence of hunger among its citizens. It needs no stressing that the people or peoples of a country cannot be healthy and disease-free unless they are able to have a balanced diet as a result of self-sufficiency. It is certainly the duty of the government to guarantee that the people, of whom they are the rulers, are able to survive without receiving assistance from others. If the people of a country are condemned to live by begging, then the government deserves to be condemned.

Though it is the primary duty of the government to see that none of its citizens are forced into slavery for want of food, it is the duty of ordinary individuals also to relieve the pain of poverty in the society. That could be achieved by the people of the country working assiduously to increase its material wealth, and also by the affluent citizens sharing their extra wealth with those that are not so affluent.

Generally speaking, there are two main categories of people who really suffer from starvation. One category is those who cannot work physically or mentally at all, due to their physical or mental disabilities. The other category is the ascetics, the orphans and the aged. It is the duty of the moneyed people to protect these two categories of people from starvation. In fact it is in such socially, morally and religiously commendable actions that a wealthy person should invest his savings.

There is another category of starving people who are strong and able bodied and are willing to work, but they cannot find work. There is no one to give them work, and the good lady called the "Land" cannot ridicule them by saying that they are only pretending to be indigents, because the "Land" knows that they don't own any land to cultivate. These people also starve and are, in consequence, forced to beg. The ruler should not allow such a situation to develop. If he permits such things to happen, then such a ruler must be condemned.

The duty of the ruler should be to remove the distinction between the haves and the have-nots by abolishing the inequalities in society. It would not be wrong to say that there is more money in the hands of the individual citizens than in the treasury of a country. It is incumbent on the ruler tactfully to channel this private money for the benefit of the society. This channelling should not involve force or compulsion. It should be done through persuasion.

There is a chapter in the Tirukkuṟaḷ called "Oppuravu" which literally means levelling, or the removal of disparity or imbalance. "Oppuravu" is the act of the moneyed sharing their wealth with the non – moneyed, rather than the non - moneyed going to the moneyed to receive bounties, or the government forcing the moneyed to part with their surplus wealth. "Oppuravu" means giving without expecting anything in return. To give because of external pressure or fear or threat is not "Oppuravu".

Just like the clouds pouring their water on the land and on the rivers and on the seas, if the affluent people give away their surplus to the destitute who are able bodied and are willing to work hard, then those that are not affluent will work hard and the country will become self-sufficient.

This is the economic principle which Tiruvaḷḷuvar has advocated in the Tirukkuṟaḷ. Now look at the English translation of the Tirukkuṟaḷs discussed above.

"All the resources that men of worth take pains to accumulate should be put to use in doing good to others."

(Tirukkuṟaḷ - 212)

"A proper country is one that runs without besetting famine, constant disease or bitter enemies."

(Tirukkuṟaḷ - 734)

"A region that, in terms of wealth, is self-sufficient deserves to be called a country".

(Tirukkuṟaḷ - 739)

Episode 23

WILL YOU PUNISH YOUR OWN BODY?

Nāladiyār is an anthology of four hundred ethical verses which are didactive in effect. The poetic painting contained in verse No.226 is beautiful and memorable. The message conveyed through this poetic painting is an ideal balm to those whose minds are instantly blinded when they are angered by others. When we are angry, the faculty of reasoning recedes and the feeling of vengeance comes to the fore. This results in our becoming temporarily insane. But as most of us fail to realize this truth, the Nāladiyār verse tries to drive it home. The verse says that it does not behove us to abandon abruptly our friends just because they have acted in a manner contrary to our expectations, interests or wishes.

It is human to err. But it is inhuman to hate a friend who has always been nice to us, and to whom we have been even nicer all these years. To illustrate this point, the author of the verse employs a superb analogy. It is this. Your hands are more precious to you than a bosom friend. Life will be miserable to anyone without their hands. One's brain coordinates its functions in such a way that there is hardly any confusion about the various functions performed by the various organs and limbs of the body. Even so there are occasions when our own finger pokes our eye unwittingly. The poke may be so bad as to require medical attention or hospital treatment. Perhaps at its worst, the poke might even result in the eye being left permanently blind; still no one thinks of punishing the finger by chopping it off. For, we know that it is this very finger which unwittingly poked the eye that also rushes to cup it and rub it to soothe its pain and wipes away its tears.

Relations, friends and colleagues are expected to behave in the same way as shown in the above illustration. Conflicts do arise; misunderstandings do occur. But they should not be nursed; they should not be harboured. It is only when we forget and forgive that we become great; it is then that we elevate ourselves above the ordinary.

Oh! king of the mountains,
where the bamboo grows sky high!
Can it be right to forsake your life-long friends
even when they do you wrong?
Will you cut off your finger,
if by accident it pokes you in the eye?

(Nāladiyār – 226)

In this connection it is worth remembering what the Tamil poetess Avvaiyār said about the anger of the great and noble in one of her poems the translation of which runs thus.

When anger disrupts your friendship with a worthless fellow,

it is like a crack in the rock.
It can never be put together again.
But when anger disrupts your friendship
with other kinds of people
it is like a crack in a golden bangle.
If you heat it up and beat it,
it can be mended.
But, an arrow shot across the surface of a lake
though will cause a line of ripples for a moment
yet will vanish immediately.
No less quickly fades away
the anger of the upright.

(Avvaiyār)

Let us think of Nāladiyār and Avvaiyār when we are tossed in the turbulent ocean of anger and vengeance.

Episode 24

MAKE HAY WHILE THE SUN SHINES

"He that crushes cane to extract the sugar
sheds no tears when the pulp is burnt to ashes.
So too the wise man labours hard
to fulfil the purpose of his life on earth;
and when the time comes to leave it
he will shed no tears."

Nāladiyār is an ancient collection of four hundred didactic verses contained in a larger anthology called Patiṉeṇkīḻkkaṇakku (Eighteen later poems). This collection is said to have been authored by Jain poets. In its literary status, it is comparable to the Tirukkuṟaḷ. It was so highly regarded by poets of the calibre of Avvaiyār that she coined the expression Nālum Iraṇdum Collukku Uṟuti, (the four lined Nāladiyār and the two lined Tirukkuṟaḷ contain valuable words). The above verse from Nāladiyār occurs in the chapter on Impermanence. It would appear that there was a time in the history of the Tamils when they held a dislike for Nāladiyār because it harped ad nausea on the concept of transience. This was because people failed to realise that Nāladiyār contained many other acceptable teachings of great importance also.

If we pause for a minute, we will not fail to realise that the concept of transience (impermanence) is indeed a truth of which one has to be aware. While the thrust of the verses in the Nāladiyār may be to emphasise the notion of impermanence, Nāladiyār also seeks to teach many other virtues and desirable things in life. Thus it speaks of the importance of good friendship, the need for hard work, the need for saving and the need for a happy married life.

Nāladiyār is best known not only for the subject matter it deals with, but also for the artistic manner in which that subject matter is handled and for the beautiful figures of speech employed to convey the message. The verse under consideration is a classic example. Let me explain the message of the verse in the form of a decorative story:

It was a good year for the farmers. The rain did not disappoint them. It was most advantageous to the cultivators of sugar cane. A particular cane plantation at the outskirts of a village was growing luxuriantly. When the owner of the farm went to inspect his plantation one Friday, he was very pleased. He was confident that the yield of sugar cane would make him one of the richest men in the village. However, when he returned to the plantation on the following Monday he was shocked. Children of the village had trampled all over the crops and made off with many of the canes. The fact that many sugar canes had been cut and taken away did not worry him so much as the fact that many canes had been trampled and broken so as to be of no use to any one. He was so worried that he grieved within himself saying “what will be my fate, if every passer-by removes a cane every time they pass this way?”. To him, each cane appeared to be so dear and important that he did not like any one touching them, let alone taking them away. Though he himself had wanted to have a taste of the sugar, yet he controlled himself and refrained from touching even a single cane. He derived satisfaction from simply looking at the plantation which was so green and verdant.

A poet of the village who chanced to go that way on that Monday noticed the frustration of the owner. Seeing the ruined state of the plantation, he well understood the owner’s exasperation; chuckling to himself, he went on his way.

A month or so later, the very same poet had occasion to pass by the same sugar cane plantation. Now the scene had totally changed. The sugar canes had been harvested and the land was stripped of any vegetation. Instead, there were tens of people, some crushing the sugar canes and others boiling the juice in large pots for treacle after the juice had been expressed. The refuse of the very sugar canes which the owner of the land could not bear to see despoiled a month ago, was now being piled up as waste pulp. It was no more recognisable as sugar cane; and the owner of the plantation himself felt no concern for the waste pulp. Exposed to the elements, the piles of waste pulp were drying in the scorching sun.

The owner did not want all that discarded fibre to go waste, and so he came round and ordered the women who were preparing treacle to heap the waste pulp on the open fire to heat the pots containing the fresh juice. What an ironical scene it was! The poet was surprised. It was the very same person who got exasperated when he saw his sugar cane plantation vandalised a month ago, that now happily ordered the working women to put the waste pulp into the fire, without any sense of remorse.

The scene which that village poet witnessed on that occasion would have been witnessed by the villagers also year after year without provoking any reflection. But that scene made the poet think and out of his reflection this verse was born. The scene which the poet witnessed at the harvest field made the poet think of the wise and the enlightened. The enlightened do not fear death; nor mourn when it occurs. The enlightened are people who make full use of their body when it is hale and hearty. When the body has lost its use and the soul is ready to depart the body, they do not grieve.

When the sugar cane was ready to produce its yield, the owner of the plantation took every precaution to protect it, and to ensure that full benefit was obtained from it. However once the expected benefit had been garnered, he did not hesitate to throw the refuse into the fire.

The moral of the verse is this. Before the sugar cane is discarded as fibrous waste you must extract the juice, prepare your treacle and molasses. Likewise before the youthful body becomes old and dies, you must make use of it to realise the ultimate.

This thought may not appeal to the present world which is more materialistic than ever before, but still it is worth pondering, is it not?

Let us now have a second look at the Nāladiyār verse in translation.

He that crushes cane to extract the sugar,
sheds no tears when the pulp is burnt to ashes.
So too the wise man labours hard
to fulfil the purpose of his life on earth;
and when the time comes to leave it,
he will shed no tears.

(Nāladiyār -35)

Episode 25

MOTHER IS THE GREATEST

Nānmaṇikkadikai is one of the eighteen anthologies included in the larger collection of didactic poems called Patiṉeṇkīḻkkaṇakku. Literally "Nānmaṇikkadikai" means four gems. It is so called because each one of the poems has four pieces of advice. There are one hundred and six poems in Nānmaṇikkadikai. The author of this ethical work is known as Viḷampi Nākaṉār. It is believed that the author was a worshipper of Lord Krishna.

The verse relating to this episode is verse No. 57 of Nāṉmaṇikkadikai. This particular verse has been chosen because it contains some thoughts which are relevant to the current state of moral decay in the West as well as in the East. At the present time human relationship is in the decline. The cement that used to hold people together appears to have rotted and lost its adhesiveness. Wherever you look, the family bond and social links seem to have grown loose or to have disintegrated altogether. Day in and day out, you hear and read of filial ingratitude, parental irresponsibility, conjugal infidelity, breach of trust and disdain for God. The result is that there is no stability in society, and there is no peace or happiness in the home. In an effort to mend matters, politicians have started to insist that there will be no way forward unless society goes back to its roots and basics. Church leaders also have joined the politicians in trying to dissuade the people from going haywire in the name of liberty and freedom of choice.

Verse No. 57 enumerates four great and valuable things in the world. The translation of the verse runs like this.

There is no member of the body more valued than the eye;
no one is more important to a woman than her husband;
nothing is more precious than your children;
but when it comes to your mother,
not even God comes into the reckoning!

(Nāṉmaṇikkadikai – 57)

Anybody who is familiar with the literary works of Avvaiyār, the great Tamil poetess, would be reminded of one of her poems, which speaks in almost the same vein. She says:

"The pleasure of being fed with love and affection will be gone once one's mother is gone; the advantage of getting the best of education and learning will go with the demise of one's father; a life of comfort and confidence will become eroded once one's kith and kin have gone or parted ways; the feeling of valour and bravery will disappear the moment one becomes brotherless; but the day your wife departs all that you reckoned great and pleasurable would be gone." No wonder great minds of different times thought alike. This is because truth is eternal.

Episode 26

SELFLESS DEER PARTNERS

In the history of Tamil literature those works that are didactic or moral in nature are referred to as Patiṉeṇkīḻkkaṇakku. The name itself means that it is a collection of eighteen pieces of work. Of those eighteen pieces five are anthologies of love poems. They are:

1. Aintiṇai Aimpatu;
2. Aintiṇai Eḻupatu;
3. Tiṇaimoḻi Aimpatu;
4. Tiṇaimālai Nūṟṟaimpatu and;
5. Kainnilai

In this episode we will look at a poetic painting from Aintiṇai Aimpatu. There are significant differences between the life of humans and that of animals. Animals, being devoid of the faculty of reasoning, do not very much express the consequences of pain or pleasure. Humans do express them very much. The realisation of those consequences affects the life of humans greatly. This feeling of consequence affects the life of the humans greatly. The world of literature is nothing but an acceptably exaggerated record of that pain and pleasure. Though there is this marked difference in the feeling of consequences of pain and pleasure between animals and humans, yet the poets in their poems portray animals as if they had all the same feelings and characteristics that are attributed to human beings. For instance, if a female partner of a monkey dies, the male partner might weep and mourn for a couple of hours or days. Thereafter that thought of loss will be out of its mind and it will choose another female partner and start life as if nothing had happened. In the case of human beings that will not be the case. A woman who has lost her husband or a man whose wife has died will not forget the bereavement so easily. More often than not, she or he would desist from marrying again and continue her or his life as a widow or widower, concentrating on the welfare of their young children. The death of the spouse will be commemorated every year until the survivor's death, after which the children will continue to commemorate it until they die. At least, this is the general practice among Tamils even today. Of course there are exceptions.

Animals do not appear to have such practices. Nevertheless, poets attribute such noble and laudable human qualities to animals also. Poems of the Tamil classical age are replete with such poetic imaginations and exaggerations. Such imagery in the poems serves as a brilliant background to highlight the main theme of the poems. Here is a painting from Aintiṇai Aimpatu. The eyes of a girl and a boy met, and the heart of each entered the heart of the other. The boy wanted to go far away to make money so that they could lead a happy married life.

The girl did not like even temporary separation; but as a male, the boy's mind was set on his goal. Having given assurances that he would return soon to marry her, he left on a long journey on a road passing through forests. The girl continued to worry, entertaining the fear that her handsome lover might be enticed by another girl in a distant land. Her maid praised the qualities of the boy and consoled her, saying that the jungles he would pass through are full of scenes and incidents which would make him continuously feel for her all the time. To drive home what she said, she recounted the following episode of a pair of deer in the forest and consoled her:

There was severe drought in the forest. Plants withered and ponds dried up. Animals were thirsty and were going from place to place in search of water, mistaking mirages for lakes. A doe and a stag were also there among the animals that were meandering around in search of water. After walking miles and after endless hopes and disappointments, the two deer were lucky to chance upon a small ditch of water. Both of them rushed towards it. As they approached the ditch, the stag realised that the water in the ditch was very shallow and that it would not be sufficient to slake the thrirst of even one. The same realisation dawned on the doe also. A thought flashed through the mind of the stag which went like " if I tell my partner that the water in the ditch is not sufficient for both of us and that she alone should drink whatever is available, she would not listen. Therefore the best thing would be for me to pretend to drink; so that my partner will then drink the water and quench her thirst".

So thinking, the stag reached the ditch together with its partner, lowered its head to the level of the water as his partner did, and pretended to drink.

They were there quite for some time in that position. Still the water level did not go down. Suspecting that there must be something funny happening, the stag lifted its head and looked towards the doe and their eyes met. It then dawned on him that the doe also had entertained the same self sacrificing thought as he had, and that she also was only pretending to be drinking. In the process neither of the deer drank a drop of water.

They were mere animals; but they loved each other so much that each one was prepared to sacrifice its needs for the needs of the other. Such incidents are commonplace in the jungle which your lover will be passing through. Your lover in his journey will be watching scenes like this and such sights will intensify his love towards you. He will never forget you. He will accomplish his mission as soon as possible and return to you. Therefore don't you worry my dear girl. In this way her maid consoled her mistress.

Here is the translation of that poem.

I have heard them say this often.
Please listen my friend.
When there is only a little water to be had in the forest,
they say that the stag only pretends to drink,
so that the doe may drink her fill
without worrying about him.
That is the path your lover chose to walk.

(Aintiṇai Aimpatu-38)

Episode 27

THE NOBILITY OF NON-COVETING

Nations all over the world have a grammar for their language. The Tamil nation is perhaps the only nation that has not only a detailed grammar for its language, Tamil, (which is the most ancient living language of India), but also has a grammar for human conduct. The Tolkāppiyam, the oldest of the Tamil classics dating back to the third century before Christ, is such a grammar. The Tirukkuṟaḷ which followed the Tolkāppiyam is a work of grammar of human conduct which is easy to understand though not so easy to follow. Chapter 15 of the Tirukkuṟaḷ has as its heading "Not coveting the wife of another".

It was the view of Tiruvaḷḷuvar that the folly of coveting another's wife cannot be found among those that know the meaning of righteousness. In one of his Kuṟaḷs, in Chapter 15, he says that the noble manliness of not looking into the eyes of another's wife is not only a virtue of the wise but also a mark of exemplary conduct. This may be dismissed as a grammatical notion that is difficult to follow. But in Tiṇaimālai Nūṟṟaimpatu there is a poem which illustrates a scene where the man conducts himself in such an exemplary manner. Let us now enjoy the scene:

A boy and a girl loved each other, but parental control prevented them from getting married with their parents' blessings. So the boy and the girl reluctantly decided to elope, so that they could get married on their own accord and start a new life in a far off town. The boy and the girl planned it well; yet the parents of the girl got wind of the elopement and they sent the girl's maid to fetch them back, promising that they would now agree to their marriage.

The maid pursued them post haste. On the way, she saw a middle aged couple coming on foot from the opposite direction; and the maid asked of the man whether they by any chance had seen a young couple on their way. The couple looked at each other and their eyes spoke. The man replied in the affirmative. "Yes" he said, "I saw a cheerful young lad bright as the sun, pass me on the way; and my wife tells me that she saw a girl following the boy serene as the moon. They must be the couple you are seeking. If that couple are near and dear to you, please hurry up and then you may succeed in catching up with them."

What we learn from the poem is that as a married man the male speaker did not look at the female partner of the young couple that was eloping.

It was only his wife not the man who looked at the female partner and observed her beauty. It is this quality of a man which Tiruvaḷḷuvar described as *Piṟaṉ Maṉai Nōkkāta Pērāṇmai.*

The poem may be translated thus.

I saw a man radiant as the sun;
my wife says she saw a girl radiant as the moon.
Go after them quickly,
and if they are the pair you seek,
your aim will be achieved.

(Tiṇaimālai Nūṟṟaimpatu – 89)

Episode 28

HE IS HERE IN YOU

Some people believe in the existence of God, others do not. This is nothing new. Because it is impossible to prove that God exists, some people say that there is no God. Some people rightly or wrongly believe that God exists even though they are not able to see God. Some are in a state of confusion; some are agnostic; yet others again are atheistic.

It is unfortunate that even in this scientific age, people rush to conclusions without doing the appropriate experiment and research required for it. We are prepared to work hard for at least four years to obtain a university degree; six years for a medical degree; eight years for a doctoral degree. We don't see any problem in waiting for twenty-five years to see the first fruits of a palmyrah palm. In other words, we are ready to work for long years to achieve degrees and are ready to wait twenty five years to reap the benefit of planting a palmyrah seed; but we are not prepared to work hard to realise God the Almighty. Without working hard and without having the patience required, we rush to conclude that there is no God.

Unlike our forefathers who were prepared to believe everything that their seniors said, today's generation questions everything. They want logic even in spiritual matters which transcend the arena of science and logic. God is an area into which the light of logic cannot penetrate. It is only the light of feeling or the x-ray of love that can penetrate the fortress of God. Those who don't feel, but rationalise cannot realize God. God cannot be seen; but still he can be realised. This is what all the religions of the world tell us.

If I say to my students that three and four make seven, they are prepared to accept it. But in the area of religion, morality or spirituality, if I tell them that Tiruvaḷḷuvar has said "if you do harm to others in the forenoon, harm will certainly visit you in the afternoon (Tirukkuṟaḷ 319)", they are not prepared to believe it. They don't believe it because I am not able to prove that a person who commits an offence in the morning will himself be a victim of an offence in the afternoon.

What you see in your day to day life also does not appear to prove the Tirukkuṟaḷ I have quoted above. Day in and day out, you see a world where rascals thrive while the virtuous suffer pain. I may exhaust all my powers of persuasion to convince you that eventually virtue will be triumphant, by expounding the karmic theory of the Hindus. But you are impatient and are not prepared to believe in a future birth of which you are not sure.

It might well be that when people acquire wisdom rather than mere knowledge or information, or when people begin to listen to their heart rather than their head, or when people become more responsible for their acts, or when people acquire a true sense of right and wrong, people will believe in what Tiruvaḷḷuvar has said. Until then, it may be difficult to convince them that there is a God.

Saint Tirunāvukkaracar, a great Saivite saint, was aware of the nature of unbelievers; he has made an attempt to convince people that God can be realised provided we are prepared to pay the price of some special labour.

Dry wood, when lit, gives us fire and light. A person who looks at a stick of firewood does not realise that there is fire in that stick. However when it is rubbed against another dry stick, it catches fire and burns. As a result of concentrated and concerted effort, we are able to see the fire in the dry stick.

A person who cursorily looks at a cup of milk may not know that there is oil in the milk in the form of butter. But the butter is not apparent, and the milk will not yield the butter easily. If you boil the milk and churn it thoroughly, then the butter will begin to coagulate and float on the surface of the watery whey. All that is needed is some effort in the form of boiling and churning.

Sparkling brilliance can be obtained from certain stones which look dull in first appearance. In the unpolished state those stones are referred to as rough diamonds. If such a stone is polished and cut in the right way by the jeweller, then you will see light radiating from it. There was that light in the unpolished rough, dull stone, but it was not clearly visible to the onlooker as long as it remained untouched and unworked. Once it has been worked upon and after some pain has been taken to look deep into it, you can see the light.

The three things, dry wood, fresh milk and unworked stone are analogies used by Tirunāvukkaracar in a Tēvāram to show that God can be realised only through serious efforts and those that don't seek God seriously can never realise God.

The Nāyaṉmārs were saints who tied themselves strongly to the Almighty and pulled him towards them with the string of pure love to realise God.

Nāvukkaracar exhorts us to do the same to realise God. No pains, no gains.

This is the Tēvāram in translation.

He is like fire in dry wood,
like ghee in milk,
like light in an uncut diamond;

in all three, he remains concealed.
If you befriend him truly,
and draw him to you with the cord of love,
he will come and stand before you.

(Tirunāvukkaracar Tēvāram -6121)

Episode 29

NO GRACE, NO SALVATION

You pour out the nectar of your grace,
but when I try to drink it down,
because of my past deeds I choke on it.
Grant to me that I may drink
of that honey-sweet, fresh-flowing stream,
then I shall live indeed.
Master, your servant languishes in deep distress;
You are my only refuge.

The above hymn is a translation of a verse from the Tiruvācakam of which the author is Saint Māṇickavācakar. "Those who don't melt for the Tiruvācakam will not melt for any other words", is an old adage; such is the greatness of the Tiruvācakam.

The theory of Karma is a cardinal belief of the Saivites. The hymnal literature of the Tamils reflects this theory at every turn. "It is the pregnant mother who has to deliver the child at the end of all whimpers and wailings" is a Tamil proverb: *A̲ḻuta̲ḻutum piḷḷai avaḷē pe̱ra vēṇdum.*

This applies equally well in relation to the salvation of souls also. In other words the consequences of the acts and deeds of the souls can be purged only by the souls themselves undergoing the consequences. There are exceptions too. A soul can escape the consequences of its acts through divine intervention; but this intervention happens very rarely and exceptionally. Saivites refer to the Almighty Siva as *Calamilan,* that is, He who has no likes or dislikes. The Almighty is like fire which has no foes or friends. If the people that are afflicted by cold go near the fire, they will be warmed; but those that do not go near it will never have their cold dispelled. Fire is always there. It is up to those who want relief from cold to approach it. It makes no difference to the fire whether you approach it or not.

God is all merciful. He continues to shower on us his grace and love. It is we who are not ready to receive it due to the load of sins which we have accumulated and from which we have not gained release. Saint Māṇickavācakar explains this predicament of the souls in a beautiful and meaningful hymn. Let us see again the English translation of the Tamil hymn.

You pour out the nectar of your grace,
but when I try to drink it down,
because of my past deeds I choke on it.
Grant to me that I may drink
of that honey-sweet, fresh-flowing stream,
then I shall live indeed.
Master, your servant languishes in deep distress;
You are my only refuge.

(Tiruvācakam –Adaikkalappattu -10)

Episode 30

DIVINE CONDUCT

The conquest of Lanka was completed with the killing of Ravana. Then, Vibeeshana retrieved Sita from the prison cell and brought her to the presence of Rama in the hope that Rama would be pleased to see her after fourteen long years. Sita fell at the feet of Rama. Instead of embracing Sita with passion, Rama uttered harsh words chastising her for having remained alive in the prison cell of Lanka, eating meat and drinking alcohol. Shocked by the caustic words of Rama, Sita became speechless. Realising that Rama was a great soul of few words, Sita decided to take her life as suggested by Rama, and asked Lakshmana to prepare a pyre.

When the pyre was lit and ready, Sita, meditating upon the Fire God and requesting Him to burn her to death if she was at fault in thought or word, plunged into the fire. Her fire of chastity was such that the burning pyre itself was destroyed by the chastity of Sita. The Fire God emerged from the fire holding Sita in the palm of His hand. Rama was shocked to watch this miracle and demanded of the Fire God who he was and why he had spared Sita. When the Fire God explained, Rama's resolve dissolved and he accepted Sita. Though Rama accepted Sita, yet the God of creation, Brahma, realised that Rama was not totally convinced by what had been said by the Fire God. So Brahma also cajoled Rama into thinking clearly.

Rama still looked a confused man. Brahma suggested to Lord Siva, the Almighty, that he make an attempt to convince Rama. Realising that, Rama was still suffering from the pangs of separation caused by the death of Dasaratha, Lord Siva signalled Dasaratha to go down from heaven to pay a visit to Rama in Lanka. Obeying the command of Lord Siva, Dasaratha came down to Lanka to meet his victorious son, who was still mourning the death of his father. The moment Rama saw Dasaratha, he fell at his feet and Dasaratha embraced Rama affectionately and uttered these words:

"The spear of promise which Kaikeyi extracted from me remained embedded in my heart even after it killed me; now upon my embracing you, it has left me. I am so pleased that I am very eager to grant you anything; please ask whatever you wish."

When Dasaratha spoke these words, Rama replied: "Father! In fact I was planning to go to heaven to see you, to seek relief for my heavy heart. But I was blessed to meet you here today to relieve my pain; what more would I need from you, my dear father!"

Even so, Dasaratha begged Rama to ask for something and Rama, falling at the feet of his father, replied as follows: "You condemned my god-like mother Kaikeyi and your son Bharatha as evil, and ostracized them. Now please grant me the boon of restoring Kaikeyi as my mother and Bharatha as my brother."

No sooner had Rama uttered these words than all the living beings of the world opened their mouths and acclaimed Rama tumultuously, says Kampaṉ, the author of Kamparāmāyaṇam, the Tamil version of the Ramayana.

Kaikeyi was the lady who had been the cause of all the trials and tribulations which Rama, Sita and Lakshmana underwent for a period of fourteen years in the jungle. If there was anybody whom Rama could not pardon, it was Kaikeyi. Notwithstanding this, when there came an opportunity to reunite the family torn apart by Kaikeyi's unseemly conduct, Rama snatched the opportunity and made his magnanimous request. This request of Rama is something beyond the nature of ordinary humans. But when Rama did that which Tiruvaḷḷuvar has exhorted us to do in his Tirukkuṟaḷ (namely to punish people who have caused you trouble by doing them good so as to make them feel ashamed of their conduct), the fauna and flora of the universe loudly expressed their pleasure by singing Rama's praise.

The verse of Kampaṉ which enshrines this particular episode is a beautiful masterpiece demonstrating the pinnacle of culture Kampaṉ wanted the Tamils to achieve. Here is the direct translation of that verse.

"Make at least one request," said Dasaratha.
The handsome Rama knelt and asked,
"Grant to me that my godly mother Kaikeyi
and Bharatha your son
whom you have disowned
may become my mother and my brother again."
Then all living creatures rose,
lifted up their voice,
and rejoicing sang Rama's praise.

(Kamparāmāyaṇam-4020)

Episode 31

NEED NOT THE BRIDEGROOM HAVE A PERSONALITY?

These are days when men are told ad nauseam that a woman is in no way second to a man, and that women and men should enjoy parity of status in all areas of human activity. These are also days when Tamil writers write a lot about feminism and empowerment of women. In their attempt to liberate the "enslaved" Tamil women, the Tamil writers miss no opportunity to condemn the poets and poetesses of yore. Even Avvaiyār, the Tamil poetess who is a household name, has not been spared. This episode is not chosen to comment on the correctness or otherwise of those who claim to be sweating and toiling for the "empowerment" of women. The other day when the subject of Tamil womanhood came to be discussed at a wedding reception the writer was reminded of a four line verse by Avvaiyār, which throws some light on what Avvaiyār thought of the rights of the women of her times.

As many Tamil readers may know, Avvaiyār was a spinster who dedicated her entire life to the cause of Tamil language and literature. Avvaiyār was always on the move. She was an itinerant. One day she chanced to be at a temple where a Hindu wedding was in progress. Avvaiyār was not one of the invited guests at the wedding. As she chanced to be at the temple, her attention was drawn to the ceremony that was going on in connection with the wedding. At the *Maṇamēdai* (matrimonial altar) the bridegroom, who was lean, emaciated and sullen looking, was seated together with the *Tōḻaṉ* (best man). The officiating priest was chanting the mantras in Sanskrit, the meaning of which he himself scarcely understood. Meanwhile the bridegroom sat there as though lifeless, like a motionless crane on the sea shore waiting for the opportunity to catch a proper fish.

The physiognomy of the bridegroom revealed that he was not only not handsome but also that he was a senseless ignoramus. All of a sudden there was a hustle and bustle, and from the side emerged the bride bedecked in a gorgeous *Kāñcipuram* silk saree, with jasmine fragrance emanating from the floral garland round her neck. Having made their way through the disorderly congregation, the bride and the flower girls reached the podium where the bridegroom was sitting, showing no sign of life or excitement.

The officiating priest resumed his chanting and after the bride had performed a couple of ceremonial ablutions, standing-ups, sitting-downs and bending-overs, the young women who were in attendance on the bride softly and slowly removed the veil that until that moment was covering her face.

The sunken yet piercing eyes of Avvaiyār fell on the bride whose face revealed that she was the epitome of knowledge and beauty. Her eyes, forehead, nose and lips glowed with life and energy without compromising her modesty.

All those who had gathered there were appreciating and admiring one aspect or another of the bride's bewitching beauty. The bridegroom still sat there stoically displaying neither joy nor sorrow. They were a perfect mismatch. Whoever had been the person who had horoscopically matched them together, Avvaiyār could not allow the marriage to be accomplished. She burned with fury. She decided that the wedding should not be allowed to be completed. So she went to the altar where the officiating priest was about to solemnize the matrimony and thundered thus:

"Stop this! Who arranged this marriage? Who was the astrologer who said that these two were fit to be married as husband and wife? The astrologer is wrong. If the God of creation has ordered this, he is also wrong. These two are a perfect mismatch. These two are incompatible. Where is Brahma, the creator who has already been deprived of one of his five heads? If it was he who ordained that this bridegroom who is no better than a piece of dead wood should be given in marriage to this beautiful girl, if I catch him, I will cut off his four remaining heads also".

It was only then that the audience and the parents of the girl realised that the bridegroom was a person who lacked personality and that his marriage to the girl could result in her eternal misery. Nevertheless the wedding went ahead and Avvaiyār left the place hurt and chagrined. Let us now see the translation of the verse attributed to Avvaiyār:

"If only I could get hold of the Brahma who ordained the marriage of this deer of a girl to this dry log of a man, I would wring his four necks and cut off his four heads so that they go the same way as the fifth one which Lord Siva has already dealt with."

If only I could get hold of Brahma,
I would wring his necks
until his four remaining heads fell off,
just as Siva did to the fifth one,
for arranging the marriage of this innocent girl
with that old stick of a man!

[Avvaiyār Pādal]

Episode 32

THE PERSONIFICATION OF VERACITY

The story of Ariccantiran transformed Mohandas Karamchand Gandhi into Mahatma Gandhi. This story is not native to Tamil Nadu. But the Tamil version of the story in the form of Ariccantira Purāṇam was born in Tamil Nadu. This masterly work was created by a poet called Vīra Kavirāyar. Even though the nucleus of the story was borrowed from North India, the work of Vīra Kavirāyar has surpassed the original in every respect, just as Kamparāmāyaṇam of Kampaṉ of Tamil Nadu is considered to be head and shoulders above the Ramayana of Valmiki of North India.

Way back in Sri Lanka, children who are initiated into Tamil literature used to be taught works like Ātti Cūdi, Koṉṟai Vēntaṉ, Mūturai, Nal Vaḻi, Nanneṟi, Ariccantira Purāṇam, Naḷa Veṇpā, Kusēla Upākkiyāṉam, Kamparāmāyaṇam and Villi Pāratam. It is the sheer beauty of their form and content that made Tamil teachers choose those works as suitable texts for teaching Tamil literature to their children. Ariccantira Purāṇam narrates the story of a person who underwent untold hardships as a result of remaining steadfastly truthful in severely trying situations.

There is a verse from the Ariccantira Purāṇam, which portrays Ariccantiraṉ's stead-fastness in a beautiful way. Before the readers have a taste of the contents of that particular verse, it is desirable to have an idea of the circumstances leading to the ideal which it depicts.

Intiraṉ, the Lord of the Heavens held a grand party for the various sages of the Heavens. While the party was in progress, Intiraṉ asked the assembly whether they had known any king in the world who was a personification of all conceivable virtues. Vaciṭṭaṉ who was the greatest among the sages (Bramma Rishi), told Intiraṉ without hesitation that Ariccantiraṉ, the king of Hastinapuri, was such a person of impeccable qualities. Sage Vicuvāmittiraṉ who was an arch rival and enemy of sage Vaciṭṭaṉ intervened, and said that Arichchandran was an embodiment of vice and that he could disprove the statement of sage Vaciṭṭaṉ.

There followed an altercation between Vaciṭṭaṉ and Vicuvāmittiraṉ. Intiraṉ intervened and asked both the sages what they would agree to do in the event of either of them being proved wrong. Vaciṭṭaṉ had no doubts whatsoever about the sterling qualities of Ariccantiraṉ. So he said that he would proceed in the direction of the god of death (Yamaṉ) carrying a pot of palm wine (which act was thought to be a demeaning act proper only for wicked and base people) and that he would strip himself of all the psychic powers he had acquired over the years and which had earned for him the title of Bramma Rishi.

Vicuvāmittiraṉ in turn promised that he would part with a half of all his psychic attainments in the event of his failing to prove what he had said of Ariccantiraṉ.

From then on, Vicuvāmittiraṉ contrived all manner of deceits to make Ariccantiraṉ tell a lie. The machinations of Vicuvāmittiraṉ resulted in Ariccantiraṉ losing his crown as well as his wife Cantiramati and his son Lōgitācan. Eventually Ariccantiraṉ, Cantiramati and Lōgitācan became slaves. A funeral-undertaker in the employ of the king, who belonged to the lowest of social castes, enslaved Ariccantiraṉ and employed him at the cemetery to burn the dead bodies brought there.

Vicuvāmittiraṉ plotted for Cantiramati to be accused of the murder of the king's son. The king condemned her to death and she was taken to the cremation ground to be cut in two with a sword. It fell on Ariccantiraṉ to perform the execution of Cantiramati. Ariccantiraṉ hesitated, but Cantiramati importuned him to do his duty. Ariccantiraṉ seated Cantiramati on a firm seat and prepared to cut her body in two with his sword. Vicuvāmittiraṉ rushed to the scene and said to Ariccantiraṉ: Oh, foolish Ariccantiraṉ! Even at this stage you can spare the life of your wife. All that you have to do is to tell a small lie; say that you did not promise your kingdom to me." Ariccantiraṉ and Cantiramati remained steadfast and the chagrined Vicuvāmittiraṉ asked in exasperation:

"Ariccantiraṉ! Don't you regret that you have lost your kingdom? Don't you regret that your son Lōgitācan has died? Does it not perturb you that you have been deprived of all your possessions? Don't you worry that you are going to lose even your future bliss."

Ariccantiraṉ and Cantiramati answered that they were not at all worried about all those losses. Stunned by their reply, Vicuvāmittiraṉ asked why, and the couple with one voice replied: "These things do not hurt us because we are proud not to have gone back on our promise." Unable to believe the adamantine steadfastness of Ariccantiraṉ to his virtue of veracity, Vicuvāmittiraṉ disappeared from the scene accepting his defeat. Here is the translation of that verse containing their incredible replies.

"We lost our kingdom,
our son, and all our wealth.
We only hope that there will be
a place for us in heaven.
Even if that too is lost,
never would we dare to tell a lie."
At that, chagrined and speechless,
Vicuvāmittiraṉ vanished.

(Ariccantira Purāṇam – 130)

Episode 33

A DECEPTIVE BEETLE

It was a coastal village replete with blueberries called *Nāvalpaḻam* in Tamil. Potable water was available only at springs in a few places. Those who lived in areas where the water was saline, used to walk great distances the pots on their heads to good water areas to fetch water. A beautiful village girl set out in the early morning with a pot to fetch water from a nearby spring which belonged to a temple.

As she was walking underneath a blueberry tree, she saw a dark, round object on the ground. Thinking that it was a ripe blueberry, she put the pot down and picked it up to see whether it was fully ripe. She placed the "fruit" on her right palm and turned it over to inspect it. In fact it was not a blueberry. It was a black beetle. The beetle tried to recover from the shock of being picked up, and started to move slowly across the girl's palm.

Her palm was so soft and tender that the beetle thought that it was walking on the petals of a lotus flower. So thinking, the beetle looked up and saw the beautiful, radiant face of the girl. The lustre in her face made the beetle conclude that the face of the girl was the moon in its fullness. Even as it came to that conclusion, the clever beetle was gripped by fear. As the moon can be seen only at night, the beetle concluded that it must be nightfall, and feared that the flower might close at any moment and ensnare it. So without further delay, the beetle flew away.

The little girl picked what she thought was a blackberry,
but in fact it was a beetle.
So soft was the palm of her hand,
the beetle thought it was a lotus flower.
As it looked around for the nectar.
it chanced to see her moonlike face;
and, in fear that the lotus flower would close
when it saw the moon rise,
at once it took wing and flew away.

(Ta̲nippādal)

NOTE:

It is common knowledge that many flowers open when the sun rises, and close when the sun sets and the moon comes out. The imaginative composer of this poem has attributed human wisdom and cleverness to the beetle. It is customary in Tamil literature to compare the hands and fingers of ladies to flower petals and their faces to the full moon.

Episode 34

MISERIES NEVER COME SINGLY

Misfortunes always come together; they follow one after the other. It never rains, but it pours. No one knows why; it is inexplicable. Hence the English proverb "misfortunes never come alone". This has been the case throughout the ages. A Tamil poet of great sagacity has composed a poem narrating the predicament of a person who was subjected to a series of miseries within a short spell. Before seeing the poem, let us see how the misery of the person unfolds.

There was a farmer who was very poor. Though poor, he was very enterprising and tried very hard to make ends meet. The rains failed and prevented him from cultivating his farm. He was eking out a bare existence with no savings for a rainy day. Of course he had petty debts as well.

One day, after a long spell of drought, all of a sudden, it started to rain cats and dogs. This made the farmer very happy. It was the dead of the night. Still he could not sleep. His mind then started to make plans and he decided to sow the paddy seeds in his field early the next morning. He brought down the stock of seed paddy from the loft and poured the required amount into a gunny bag. As he was doing that, he heard the plaintive bellow of his cow in the cow shed. Wondering why it was making such a noise he rushed to the cowshed only to see the cow flat on the ground, suffering from labour pain while the calf was gradually coming out of the mother's womb. He attended to the needs of the cow and the calf, and returned to the house to convey the good news to his wife who was still in bed. As he entered the front room of the mud house, he heard a thud only to find that a side-wall of the front room had collapsed due to flood water. His heart sank into his shoes.

Fearing that he would be delayed if he were to start attending to the fallen wall, he ran into the house to tell his wife that their cow had given birth to a calf. As he opened the bedroom, the sight he saw there gave him a rude shock. He found his wife wailing and moaning due to labour pain. This was unexpected because the Ayurvedic physician had told him that it would be four weeks before she delivered the baby. He comforted his wife and rushed next door to request the elderly lady and her sister to come and attend to her needs. They came quickly and attended to his wife. Next, he hastened to his farm with the bag of seed paddy. As he left the house, he met a funeral announcer announcing the death of one of his relatives. Despite the fact that this was an ill omen, he rushed towards the field. As he neared the field, one of his creditors accidentally met him and demanded immediate payment of the debt he was owed, threatening to sue him if it was not settled forthwith. The farmer somehow bought some time, entered the field and completed the job of sowing the seed paddy.

At length he returned home with a sigh of relief, eager to know whether his wife had safely delivered the baby. As he stepped into his house the sight of some unexpected guests threw him into a state of dejection because he was unable to entertain them. He welcomed them with a false smile and went into his back yard to pluck some vegetables and fruits. While in the garden, a viper which had been flushed out of its hole by the rain waters bit him. The guests who were there made arrangements to take him to a snakebite specialist when the sheriff of the king arrived to demand the quarterly tax. As if all these miseries were not enough to force him to commit suicide, the priest of the village temple came with his retinue to ask for alms.

The above is the substance of that poem. The succession of events enumerated might sound impossible and fictitious. One might even wonder whether all these things could happen to one person in a single day. But it is not altogether impossible, is it?

Let us now see the English translation of the poem.

It had been raining cats and dogs,
and the floods swept away his house;
the cow was in labour,
his wife was sick equally,
and his servant breathed his last.
Unconcerned, he hurried off to his fields
To sow the seed before the ground dried out.
On his way, the money-lender met him,
demanding to be paid;
the post-man brought notice of another death;
guests came by whom he could not turn away;
the tax man came with a demand for his arrears;
then he was bitten by a snake.
Finally, to cap it all,
the priests turned up with a plea for alms.

(Ta<u>n</u>ippādal)

Episode 35

WHO IS A GOOD PERSON?

Who is a good person? Who is a bad person? Is there any criterion which will help us distinguish a good person from a bad person? Is there a yardstick with which to measure whether a person is good or not? The answer is that there is no such criterion or touch stone or yardstick. If that is so, how can one establish or continue a relationship? This question appears to have vexed the great Tiruvaḷḷuvar, the author of the Tirukkuṟaḷ also.

So in an effort to give an answer to this vexed question Tiruvaḷḷuvar composed a two line poem popularly known as a Kuṟaḷ. He says that if you are going to look for somebody who is absolutely perfect, whiter than white, you are not going to find such a person. Since that is the case, you must look at the merits of a person and at their demerits, and then weigh up the good qualities against the bad. If the good qualities outweigh the bad qualities, then accept that person as good, and vice versa.

The authors of the anthology called Nāladiyār also appear to have been confronted with a similar question on this issue of who is acceptable and who is not. They also appear to have come to almost the same conclusion, but have adopted a different approach in arriving at it.

Nāladiyār drives home the fact of life by means of an analogy. Paddy is something we like and need, but then, paddy is not rice grain pure and simple. It also has an unpalatable and an inedible substance called husk. Water is an indispensable food item for all living things. But it also has froth and bubbles which we do not need. The lotus flower is not only beautiful, but is also fragrant. But then, not all its petals are beautiful; some of them are unattractive; however those unattractive petals and sepals are part and parcel of the flower.

If we want to benefit from the rice grain, then we cannot reject the paddy saying that it also has a husk; if we want to quench our thirst then we cannot reject spring water complaining that it is frothy or bubbly. Likewise if we want to enjoy the lotus flower, then we must be prepared to accept the flower as it is, notwithstanding the fact that there are unseemly petals and sepals.

In the same way, if we have a liking for someone, then we must take him/her into our affection even though they may have certain shortcomings or unlikeable qualities.

What follows is an English translation of the Nāladiyār verse.

If you think someone is a good man,
and you are very fond of him,
even when he turns out otherwise,
you have to hold your tongue.
For the paddy has its husk,
a flower its faded petals,
and the water its scum.

(Nāladiyār – 221)

Episode 36

I FEEL SHY

Theory and practice are quite different. Although one may be acquainted theoretically with an alien culture, unless one lives that culture, or lives in it, it will be difficult to appreciate it. It is this difficulty which causes the cultural shock.

The Tamils held four qualities to be intrinsic qualities of a woman. In Tamil we call them (a) *accam*; (b) *madam*; (c) *nāṇam*; and (e) *payirppu*. They can be translated into English as timidity; simplicity; shyness; and delicacy. The intrinsic qualities are also referred to as internal beauties. It is said that it is the presence of these qualities in a woman that gives her feminity; the intrinsic qualities enhance her external beauty. Finely chiselled external features, such as a nose resembling parrot's beak, Buddha's ears, rosy cheeks, pearly lips, American teeth and a crescent-shaped forehead account only for a part of a woman's beauty. Her real beauty comes from within. Timidity, simplicity, shyness and delicacy are those inner beauties. These qualities play an important part in the way a Tamil woman behaves. It is not the intention of the writer to pretend that such intrinsic qualities are particular to Tamil women only. They are present in all women, irrespective of their race or religion.

However they differ in their degree depending on the culture or tradition the woman belongs to.

There is a beautiful verse in the anthology which is a component in the larger anthology of Caṅkam poems called Eṭṭuttokai. That verse beautifully portrays how the conduct of a girl was affected by her being overly conscious of just one of those intrinsic characteristics.

With the above introduction let us enjoy the poetic painting contained in the Naṟṟiṇai verse. It was term time. There was no school. It was all play and no work for all the school children of that village. A girl called Annam from an affluent family and her chaperone were engaged playing hide and seek on the forecourt of the house. A few metres away there was a *poon* tree from which had fallen some ripe and unripe fruit. The fruit of the *poon* tree is round and beautiful to look at and it caught the attention of the girls. They made a bet between themselves that whoever collected the most would be declared the winner. With this agreement they dashed towards the *poon* tree and hurriedly picked up as much fruit as they could, until all the fruit under the tree had been collected. Then they sat down together under the tree to count the number of fruits each one had collected.

When they finished counting, they found that both of them had collected the same amount of fruit. Since neither was happy, they decided to have a recount but still the result was the same. Consequently there was no winner or loser. Thank God. There was no ill feeling between them.

As the sun got hotter, they could not continue to play on the forecourt. So they moved to a place a little further away which was shady and cooler. They sat near a *neem* tree where the soil was soft and clean. There, they played a traditional children's game with the *poon* fruit. The game involved burying the *poon* fruit in the soil and then retrieving it. After they had been playing for sometime, Annam's mother called and they returned home with their collections of fruit. In their hurry, one of them forgot to retrieve one of the pieces of fruit she had buried in the ground.

After a few months, when the rainy season was over, the two girls chanced to wander past the shady spot where they had played with the *poon* fruit some time ago. To their surprise, they saw a seedling growing luxuriantly. They readily recognized it as the produce of the fruit they had buried during their game and accidentally left in the ground. They were amazed to see that their game had resulted in the growth of a young and beautiful sapling. From then on, they developed a strange affection for the sapling. They regularly gave it water and fertiliser and tended it as if it was a human being. When Annam's mother discovered that her daughter and the chaperone had successfully cultivated a *poon* tree and were tending it carefully, she told them that the sapling had almost become their sister, and encouraged them to tend it carefully.

Eventually, the sapling grew into a large tree, no more in need of water or manure. Still, the girls harboured the strange feeling that the *poon* tree was their sister and their sisterly affection seemed ever green and alive.

Time passed, and Annam grew up and attained the age of discretion. When she transformed into a loveable lass and reached marriageable age, commensurate with age, she began to show healthy interest in the opposite sex. She found a boy of her liking in her village, and started to court. The chaperone appeared to encourage her. The lovers met at rendezvous far away from their houses and so Annam's parents were kept in the dark.

As time moved on, Annam's mother began to notice certain changes in her daughter. It did not take her long to decipher what was going on. She did not dare to confront her daughter; so she tried to extract information from the chaperone, but without success; she began to impose a strict curfew, whereby Annam was prevented from going out frequently or spending long hours outside.

When things were proving difficult, the lovers changed venues and selected meeting places closer to Annam's house so as to avoid the attention of her mother. The chaperone always acted as the go-between. One day the boy sent word through the chaperone to meet Annam near the shady grove behind her house during the afternoon.

On the dot, the boy reached the spot and was waiting with a heavy heart. It was a hot day and the mother was having a nap. The girl and the chaperone quietly slipped away from the house to meet the boy who was waiting impatiently. When they reached the venue, Annam indicated to the chaperone to leave them and to keep watch on the movements of her mother.

The boy was seated under the *poon* tree. No sooner had the girl approached him, than he got up and gave her an affectionate hug. Although the girl enjoyed the hug, she suddenly became aware that they were showing this intimate affection in front of her sister, the poon tree, and this almost froze her, and reluctantly she pulled herself away from the boy. The boy could not understand the strange behaviour of Annam. Feeling remorseful for what she had done in the presence of the special *poon* tree she started to blush and sweat. When the boy begged her to explain her behaviour, Annam offered the explanation which is contained in the following Nar̲r̲iṇai verse.

Here is the translation.

**One day while playing
a game with poon fruit,
we buried one of them
in the soil at the playground
and totally forgot about it.
Some time later we found it germinate
and we tended the sapling
carefully with milk and butter.
As it grew up luxuriantly
our mother encouraged us
and said that it was like our sister.
What she said stuck in our mind
and we treated it as if it was indeed our sister.
Not knowing this relationship,
you have chosen this spot today
to date with me.
I feel shy to do any courting
near my sister while she watches.
You Lord of the sea shore
that bounds the sea waters
where the spiralled chanks
produce music which is
as sweet as the music of the bards!
Please avoid this spot!
There are many such secret spots around!**

(Narriṇai – 172)

Episode 37

A SNEEZE CAN CAUSE TROUBLE

All work and no play makes jack a dull boy is an age old saying. People say that it is a living adage. I don't know whether the antithesis of the saying is true. In other words, I am not sure whether it would be right to say that all play and no work will make jack a dull boy. Let us not go into details of the meaning of "work" and "play" as it would take us into uncharted waters. Kampaṉ, one of the greatest scholars in the rich firmament of Tamil literature, declared in his Kamparāmāyaṇam, through its hero Rama that pleasure can be enjoyed only when one has the experience of pain. The shade of trees under which people take refuge, is generally taken for granted. It is only when we are exposed to the scorching heat of the burning sun that we value the shade. This is true in the case of lovers also, says Tiruvaḷḷuvar, the great sage and author of Tirukkuṟaḷ.

Part III of the Tirukkuṟaḷ is on the subject of love and has two hundred and fifty couplets. Some of these couplets subtly portray the innermost emotional feelings of lovers who are gripped by the tentacles of love. Even as exposure to sun enhances one's realisation of the importance of shade, quarrelling also in the life of lovers during their period of courtship adds delight to courting; however he hastens to add that sulking should not be overdone and that it should be like sprinkling salt into the dishes to taste; dishes without a dash of table salt will be bland, but if added in excess could lead to complications, and even high blood pressure.

With the above introduction, let us see the painting contained in one of the Kuṟaḷs. It portrays one of several ways in which a girl lover could initiate quarrelling.

The style of sulking, as described in this Kuṟaḷ, is based on the Tamil traditional belief that women are very possessive and selfish, and that they continue to harp on the age-old theory that men are biologically promiscuous, or at least more promiscuous than women.

Let us now see the context of this Kuṟaḷ. As scheduled, a girl and her boyfriend met at the prearranged place. They exchanged pleasantries and talked about this and that including the question of formally breaking the news of their love affair to their respective parents. As this conversation was in progress, umpteen thoughts criss-crossed the mind of the boy and all of a sudden he sneezed somewhat violently. The girl's concern for the boy was such that even before the sneezing stopped she wished him "Nūṟu" (long life or bless you) and he said "Thank you". But not even two seconds passed before the girl entertained an unwholesome suspicion and put a long face. The boy was perplexed.

There is a belief, almost bordering superstition, that sneezing is generated only when somebody dear and near to you but living far away thinks or speaks of you. The girl in this episode, being a creature of the society that moulded and brought her up, was naturally disturbed when her boyfriend, whom she loved intimately, sneezed. Immediately her imagination took wings and ran riot. She came to the conclusion that another girlfriend of his must have thought or spoken of him, and that was the reason why he sneezed. So, without second thoughts she asked him bluntly, "who is that pretty girl who right now is pining for you and so has made you sneeze?"

The boy was truly innocent and devoted all his attention solely to this girl. So he used all his powers of persuasion to convince her that she was wrong and that she was obstinately holding on to an ancient superstition concocted by her forebears, which has no scientific basis. But the girl wouldn't agree to be convinced and so continued to sulk. As the boy was making further efforts to convince her that she was the girl to whom he had surrendered his heart and soul, suddenly he felt that another sneeze was on its way. But in spite of strenuous efforts he was unable to suppress it. Who on earth can stop a sneeze which is reckoned as the fastest natural thing in the world, having a speed of about 167 kilometres per hour? The girl was remarkably observant and was quick to react. Even as the boy struggled to suppress the sneeze at its early stage, almost in tears, the girl cut in unkindly and said, “Now I know. Some other girl is thinking of you right now and it is because you want to hide the fact that you are flirting with her that you are unsuccessfully struggling to control your sneeze. It is useless trying to hide your infidelity. Come on; tell the truth; who is that girl? Tell me now so that I can make a decision here and now.”

What can the poor boy do? How can he prove his innocence to this girl who is seizing every opportunity to find fault with him and to continue her sulking?

When he sneezed, she feigned anger. When he tried to control the sneezing, she exploded. That seems to be the nature of possessive women. Their love can indeed be cruel. The worldly wise Tiruvalluvar has magnificently succeeded in depicting the tender and sensuous feelings of young girls tormented by love. Here is the translation of the Kuṟaḷ.

“I sneezed and she blessed me.
And in the same breath
she asked in tears
‘Who thought of you now
to prompt your sneeze?”

(Tirukkuṟaḷ – 1317)

CHAPTER 6

ERA OF CLASSICAL LITERATURE

The classical literature of the Tamils is generally referred to as Caṅkam literature. Caṅkam literally means an academy or board of scholars. The word Caṅkam finds no place in the Eṭṭuttokai or the Pattuppāṭṭu. The word occurs for the first time in a piece of literature of the 8th century AD. As stated earlier it is the Eṭṭuttokai (eight anthologies), the Pattuppāṭṭu (ten long poems) and the Tolkāppiyam which are referred to as Caṅkam Ilakkiyam or Caṅkam literature. Tolkāppiyam is a work of Tamil grammar.

The length of Caṅkam poems varies very much. The lengths range from 3 lines to over 800 lines. There were 2420 Caṅkam poems; now we have only 2381 poems. The names of the authors of 102 of them are not known. 473 poets have been known by their proper names or by some catchy phrase occurring in their poems and are responsible for 2381 poems. Out of the 473 poets who have authored most of the 2381 poems, a great poet called Kapilar composed 235 poems. Poet Ammūvaṉār has composed 127 poems. Out of the 473 known poets, 293 poets have generated only a single poem each.

The fact that there are only 2381 poems which are referred to as Caṅkam poems does not mean that there were in existence only 2381 poems. The truth is that only 2381 poems have survived floods, deluge, fire, foreign invasion, and white ants and the petty prejudices of compilers and editors. It is significant to note that many other pieces of ancient literature which could be described as Cańkam poems were destroyed or lost due to the above causes. They were also destroyed wantonly by the Tamils themselves.

The body of ancient Tamil literature which many of us now know as Cańkam poems was not known to all the Tamils of Tamil Nadu during the dark centuries (200 A.D. to 600 A.D.) known as the Kaḷappra period of Tamil history. Tamil Nadu saw a revival at the end of 6th century A.D. The Saiva saints started this revival.

After many centuries of black out, the surviving Tamil literary pieces were dramatically rediscovered in the closing years of the nineteenth century. The discovery was accidental, and two Tamil literary stalwarts were responsible for this rediscovery. One was from Jaffna, Sri Lanka, and he was C.W.Thamotharampillai (1832-1901). The other was from South India and he was U.V. Saminatha Iyer [1855 – 1942].

Tamil scholars of the 18th century who were Hindus appear to have been so fanatical as to believe that non Hindu or non religious literary works did not deserve a place in the life or history of the Tamils. The non-Hindu literary works included master pieces like the Cīvakacintāmaṇi, the Cilappatikāram and the Maṇimēkalai. The earlier eighteen anthologies comprising the Eṭṭuttokai and the Pattuppāṭṭu came under the category of non-religious (secular) literary pieces and were as a result apparently treated with indifference.

Story has it that even U.V. Saminatha Iyer was not aware of the existence of the Eṭṭuttokai, the Pattuppāṭṭu or the epics such as the Cilappatikāram and the Maṇimēkalai until he met a civil Judge called Rama Swami Mudaliyar.

The Tamil classical poems were classified on the basis of their themes (motifs) as Akam and Puṟam. Akam meaning "inner" or subjective or private, literally connotes love; "Puṟam" meaning "outer" or objective or public, literally connotes war. In other words it would be right to say that Akam poems are love poems, while Puṟam poems are poems on, bravery, kingship etc.

CHAPTER 7

ERA OF ETHICAL LITERATURE

The Tamils of the classical age loved to live a full life. They believed that the world was created for them and that they should make use of everything that was available to them in the world as long as, by so doing, they were not harming others. Any reader of classical Tamil literature will not fail to realise that the ancient Tamils, who were worshippers of Siva, delighted in sensual pleasures. They appear to have worried only about the present. The thoughts of the other world yet to come, did not trouble them much. It was the spread of Jainism and Buddhism which laid the first seeds of change in the Tamil land and which changed the outlook of the Tamils in later years.

In the history of Tamil literature, the period of about four hundred years between the second century and the sixth century after Christ is referred to as the era of ethical literature. Whereas the Tamil poets of the Caṅkam age had set their mind on expressing their feelings of love and bravery and liberality, the poets of the post Caṅkam period turned their poetic and literary skills to prescribing moral rules for a peaceful life in this world. Works of such ethical codes of conduct were called the Patiṉeṇkīḻkkaṇakku. In other words, whereas the poets of the Caṅkam age composed poems which mirrored the life of the people as they saw it, the poets of the post- Caṅkam era, instead of stating how the people of their time lived, stated rather how people should live. There was reason for the shift in the approach of the poets.

The first five hundred years after the birth of Christ was a period of pandemonium and confusion in the Tamil land. The shock that was brought on the Tamils as a result of the implanting of foreign culture and religions by the northern invaders, historically referred to as Kaḷapprās, made the Tamils lose direction and they ceased to live a life harmonious with nature to which their forefathers were accustomed. This created the dire need for codes of conduct and poets produced many literary pieces enumerating various rules of conduct. Those rules are contained in eighteen anthologies referred to as the Patiṉeṇkīḻkkaṇakku.

There are 3259 verses in the Patiṉeṇkīḻkkaṇakku, most of which are verses of four lines.

CHAPTER 8

Era of Devotional Literature

Tamils of the Caṅkam age were of the firm conviction that there was nothing wrong with people enjoying the pleasures of the senses without violating the moral order which is a must for an orderly society. This wholesome attitude of the Tamils of the Caṅkam age as portrayed in Puṟanāṉūṟu was suppressed, or almost killed by the pessimistic beliefs inculcated by the atheistic religions. Because the Tamil rulers had fallen a prey to the machinations of the leaders of the invading atheistic religions, the people also willy-nilly accepted their pessimistic beliefs. However in their heart of hearts they were constantly rebelling against the negativism which was impressed upon them.

Though the ancient Tamils had been under a foreign religious yoke for about five hundred years, and despite the ethical literature that was spawned profusely during that time, the Tamils began to realise that their embracing of the atheistic faiths had not bettered their lot. However it would not be fair to say that the Tamil people reacted only against the beliefs, dogmas and practices of the religions of the occupiers; they also reacted against the attitudes and practices of that period. Moribund rituals as well as irrational religious practices, discriminatory attitudes and class distinctions that were rife in the Hindu faith were anathema to the searching spirit of rational souls. Thus there was a crying need for a man of the soil to bring about a revolution in the way religion was approached.

As if to respond to such a cry, Tamil land produced not one but a galaxy of spiritual leaders who invented a new path called bhakti path or bhakti movement in place of the path of physical service and the path of Ñāṉam. The impact of this new path propounded by these Tamil religious leaders was profound. Whereas before their time, Hindu religion was preached and practised by the Tamils in a foreign language called Sanskrit, the Tamil spiritual leaders used the Tamil language set to Tamil music. The use of Tamil and the new path of bhakti endeared the people to these spiritual teachers.

The twelve Āḻvārs and the three chief Nāyaṉmārs and Saint Māṇickavācakar all of whom lived between the sixth and the ninth centuries after Christ, gave the Tamils the finest of mystical poetry in their own language. Āḻvārs and Nāyaṉmārs were God intoxicated souls. The Tivviya Pirapantams, the Tēvārams and the Tiruvācakam of these God intoxicated souls express the yearning of the finite human soul for the infinite Almighty and reveal the passion of the transient for the eternal and permanent. The profound concepts contained in the Tivviya Pirapantam, the Tēvārams and the Tiruvācakam are rendered in exquisite metres, and matchless simplicity and piety. There are 8250 Tēvārams of which Ñāṉacampantar contributed 4158; Tirunāvukkaracar contributed 3066 while Cuntara Mūrtti Cuvāmikaḷ contributed 1026. Tiruvācakam hymns of Saint Māṇickavācakar are 656 in number and are contained in 51 chapters. Though these divine hymns are not referred to as classical literature, they are in fact in no way inferior to Caṅkam literature. It is really unfortunate that the collectors and compilers of the ancient Tamil literature failed to give these devotional hymns the enviable place they deserved in the history of classical Tamil literature.

Apart from the Tēvārams and the Tiruvācakams, there is also another corpus of devotional work called the Tirumantiram. The Tirumantiram is the seminal text of Saiva Sittāntam. The author of the Tiruṃantiram is Tirumūlar. The work is divided into nine parts and each part is known as Tantiram. The Tirumantiram contains 3047 verses and covers a variety of subjects.

Though there is a tendency to ascribe an early date to this work, the consensus is that it belongs to a later period, 8th or 9th century after Christ.

CHAPTER 9

THE EṬṬUTTOKAI

THE EIGHT ANTHOLOGIES

The Eṭṭuttokai consists of the following:

1. Naṟṟiṇai – (400 Love poems)
2. Kuṟuntokai – (401 Love poems)
3. Aiṅkuṟu Nūṟu – (500 Love poems)
4. Patiṟṟuppattu – (100 Poems about ten Cērā Kings)
5. Paripādal – (70 Poems in praise of Gods and Rivers)
6. Kalittokai – (149 Love poems)
7. Akanāṉūṟu – (400 Love poems)
8. Puṟanāṉūṟu – (400 Poems of War and Bravery)

Out of the eight anthologies (called the Eṭṭuttokai in Tamil) five anthologies contain only poems of love. These are Akanāṉūṟu, Naṟṟiṇai, Kuṟuntokai, Aiṅkuṟu Nūṟu and Kalittokai. Akanāṉūṟu has 400 poems. The poems in Akanāṉūṟu have the greatest number of lines, the shortest poem having 13 lines and the longest having 31 lines.

Let us now see a brief description of each one of them:

1. **Naṟṟiṇai** contains 400 poems the shortest of which contains 9 lines while the longest contains 12 lines.

2. **Kuṟuntokai** also contains 401 poems. The shortest of it consists of four lines and the longest eight lines.

3. **Aiṅkuṟu Nūṟu** has 500 short poems. The shortest poem has three lines while the longest has five lines.

4. **Patiṟṟuppattu** literally means ten times ten, that is one hundred. The poems are in praise of ten Cērā kings who ruled Tamil Nadu during the classical era. Ten poems have been devoted to each of the ten kings. However the first ten and the last ten poems have been lost and only eighty poems are now available.

5. **Paripādal** is also classified as a collection of love poems. They are lyrical poems. Originally there were seventy poems.Of the seventy poems forty eight have been lost. There are only twenty two left of which a few relate to love while the rest eulogise gods, deities and rivers.

6. **Kalittokai** has 149 poems and each one is a musical piece.

7. **Akanāṉūṟu** is also known as Neduntokai. This also has 400 poems describing love episodes expressing noble sentiments. Akanāṉūṟu is divided into three divisions called Kaḷiṟṟu Yāṉai Nirai, Maṇimidai Pavaḷam and Nittilakkovai.

8. **Puṟanāṉūṟu** is an anthology mostly of war poems and gives a great deal of information relating to ancient kings and poets and philanthropists. There are 400 poems in the anthology.

CHAPTER 10

The Pattuppāṭṭu

The ten long poems

The other ancient anthology called the Pattuppāṭṭu (The ten long poems) consists of the following:

1. Ciṟupāṇaṉ Āṟṟuppadai
2. Perumpāṇaṉ Āṟṟuppadai
3. Tirumuruka Āṟṟuppadai
4. Porunar Āṟṟuppadai
5. Malaipadukadām (Kūttar Āṟṟuppadai)
6. Mullaippāṭṭu
7. Kuṟiñcippāṭṭu
8. Paṭṭiṉappālai
9. Nedunalvādai
10. Maturaikkāñci

During the Caṅkam literature period, there was in existence a literary genre called Āṟṟuppadai. Āṟṟuppadai simply means referral – the act of referring someone to another person. Āṟṟuppadai literature narrates instances of poor artistes (who had already received help and assistance from affluent benefactors or philanthropists) directing a person of their own profession or guild to the same benefactor, so that the other person also could receive the same benefit and better his position.In the ancient past, musicians and dancers had practised and preserved music and dance as a family treasure. This had continued from generation to generation. In other words, music and dance were the preserve of certain groups of people. The group whose realm was music came to be known as Pāṇar. The male musician was known as Pāṇaṉ and the female musician was known as Pādiṉi.

The group or community which practised and preserved dance as their family occupation was known as Kūttar in general. Female dancers were called Viṟaliyar while male dancers were called Kūttar. Those dancers who combined acting with dancing were known as Porunar. It was through these Pāṇar, Pādiṉiyar, Kūttar, Viṟaliyar and Porunar that the ancient Tamil arts of music, dance and drama were passed down to the succeeding generations. History has it that from the pre-Christian era until the seventh century AD this community developed and perfected the fine arts to their highest form.

It would appear that the very nature of the fine arts is such that the people who practise them care for nothing else. The result is that such fine artistes are always in a permanent state of penury. At least that appears to have been the case in the Tamil land.

Bereft of possessions or permanent homes these Pāṇar, Pādiṉiyar, Kūttar, Viṟaliyar and Porunar were homeless and always on the move. Their source of income was what the patrons of music and dance gave them in return for the performance they gave. Being always on the move they knew men and matters and were admirers of nature and beauty. Like birds that move from place to place with the change of seasons, these musicians and dancers also moved from city to city on the advice and direction of fellow musicians and dancers in search of better pastures.

It is this advice and direction which is called Āṟṟuppadai in the Tamil language. This direction is full and complete and will give a vivid description of the ruler or benefactor, his country, the hills, rivers, birds, people, their sports, their life style etc. In the process of giving such vivid descriptions, they also give a great deal of information relating to the status and quality of the fine arts of those days. Most of the Āṟṟuppadai literature is very picturesque. It would not be far from the truth to say that Āṟṟuppadai literature is nothing but musical literature.

1. Tirumuruka Āṟṟuppadai

As was stated earlier, Āṟṟuppadai was developed and preserved as a form of literature by the ancient Tamils in those days. Tirumuruka Āṟṟuppadai was composed by a poet called Nakkīrar and it has 317 lines.

This is a long poem assuming the form of helpful directions given by a devotee of Lord Murukaṉ, who already has received his blessings of Murukaṉ, to another person who is desirous of receiving such blessings. This appears to be the only literary work of devotion created during the Caṅkam age. This poem sings the praise of God. From this work, we are able to gather some information about the various Murukaṉ temples that were in existence during the time of Nakkīrar. It also tells us about the methods of worship that were prevalent at that time.

2. **Porunar Āṟṟuppadai**

This is a long poem of 248 lines, and is in praise of Karikāl Cōḻaṉ who was a great king known for his administrative as well as literary skills. The poem extols the philanthropic qualities of Karikālaṉ besides describing the soothing characteristics of music. There is a passage in the poem which describes how on one occasion an actor-cum-musician succeeded in disarming highway robbers by the power of the music he created in his lute when the highway robbers threatened his life.

3. **Ciṟupāṇaṉ Āṟṟuppadai**

There were two kinds of Pāṇaṉ Āṟṟuppadai. One was Ciṟupāṇaṉ Āṟṟuppadai and the other was Perumpāṇaṉ Āṟṟuppadai. Ciṟupāṇaṉ Āṟṟuppadai is small in terms of the number of lines it contains.

Ciṟupāṇaṉ Āṟṟuppadai has 269 lines. It is about a group of musicians called Pāṇar. The life of a Pāṇaṉ family is vividly described in this poem. The family of the Pāṇaṉ who is the hero of this poem is indescribably poor. His house is in a dilapidated condition. The walls are so old that white ants have started to build their own hills around the walls of the house. The roof of the house has not been thatched for ages, and the rafters of the house are resting in a precarious position. The kitchen has not been visited for a long time and mushrooms have usurped the hearth as their home. The poverty of the Pāṇaṉ family has affected the female dog of the Pāṇaṉ also. The dog and its pups have been starving for so long that the udder of the dog is dry, and it gets annoyed when the hungry puppies come to her to quench their thirst and hunger. These scenes are described so vividly that the reader will not be able to put down the poem once he starts to read it.

4. **Perumpāṇaṉ Āṟṟuppadai**

This also describes the life of a Pāṇaṉ family. This poem is 500 lines long. From this poem we gather detailed information about a king called Iḷantiraiyan who ruled Kāñci during the pre-Christian period. It gives us detailed information about Iḷantiraiyan's rule and about the landscape beauty of Kāñci and the life style of its people.

5. **Malaipadukadām (Kūttar Āṟṟuppadai)**

This is a poem about a family of "drama- musicians" and contains 583 lines. Malaipadukadām is also known as Kūttar Āṟṟuppadai. This long poem gives detailed information about the various musical instruments used by the drama-musicians and their life of art.

6. **Mullaippāṭṭu**

Among the poems of the Pattuppāṭṭu (the ten long poems), Mullaippāṭṭu and Kuṟiñcippāṭṭu are considered to be the best love poems. The aim of these two poems is not to eulogise a king or a philanthropist. These poems deal with the intricate and inexplicable qualities of true love. Mullaippāṭṭu has 103 lines and describes the pangs of separation of a woman lover. She eagerly awaits the return of her male lover who has gone away to a distant place on a war mission promising to return before the onset of the rainy season.

7. **Kuṟiñcippāṭṭu**

This is a love poem of 261 lines. A boy and a girl fall in love with each other without the knowledge of their parents. They start to meet at a secret rendezvous. After some time due to various obstacles, they are unable to meet as they used to. Their inability to meet worries the girl a lot and she pines away, with her body becoming weaker and weaker day after day. Not knowing the cause for it, the parents of the girl try to seek other remedies.

Fearing that unnecessary medication might result in lethal consequences, a friend of the girl intervenes and explains to the parents the cause of the girl's emaciation and brings the matter to a happy conclusion.

8. **Paṭṭinappālai**

This is also a poem of love created in the imagination of the poet. This poem gives a vivid description of King Karikālaṉ and the city of Kāvirippūm Paṭṭiṉam the capital of Cōḻa Nādu which he ruled.

This poem has 297 lines and is evidence of the ancient glory of the Tamil land. It is from this poem that we are able to gather that the ancient Tamils were great sea farers and that they were engaged in maritime trade, that there were several sea ports in the Tamil land and that traders from Greece and Rome had settlements there for purposes of their trade and commerce. That the Tamils were very fair in their transactions is illustrated beautifully in this long poem. We learn from this poem that scholars learned in various branches of knowledge were in the habit of holding public debates.

9. **Nedunalvādai**

Nedunalvādai is another beautiful love poem that arose in the imagination of a mature Tamil poet. It has 188 lines of copious description elaborating the pining of a love torn girl and her soldier boy friend.

The girl is at home and the boy is in a military camp far away from the girl. The boy had promised to return within a certain period of time. The war was protracted and he could not return as promised. Tormented by the pangs of separation, the girl prays to Kāḷi (Ko<u>rr</u>avai) for the safe return of her boy friend, who is busy at the battle field fighting the enemy. This is the essence of the story in the poem. This story is interspersed with picturesque depiction of the palace of the girlfriend, the camp of the boyfriend and the painful north wind (Vādaikkā<u>rr</u>u) that torments the boy.

10. **Maturaikkāñci**

This is the longest poem in the anthology of Pattuppāṭṭu. It has 782 lines. Pāṇdiya<u>n</u> Neduñche<u>l</u>iya<u>n</u> who was the king of Maturai is the hero of this poem. While the poem praises the administrative excellence of the king, it also instructs him on the importance of the world and human life. Through this poem we gather a great deal of information relating to the ancestors of Pāṇdiya<u>n</u> Neduñche<u>l</u>iya<u>n</u>. It also gives us a good deal of information relating to the day to day activities of the Tamil people of that time.

CHAPTER 11

THE PATINEṆKĪḺKKAṆAKKU

(THE EIGHTEEN ANTHOLOGIES)

Most of the Eighteen Anthologies are didactic works. They are:

1. Ācārakkōvai
2. Iṉṉā Nāṟpatu
3. Iṉiyavai Nāṟpatu
4. Ēlāti
5. Aintiṇai Eḻupatu
6. Kār Nāṟpatu
7. Kaḷavaḻi Nāṟpatu
8. Aintiṇai Aimpatu
9. Kainnilai
10. Ciṟu Pañca Mūlam
11. Tiṇaimālai Nūṟṟaimpatu
12. Tiṇaimoḻi Aimpatu
13. Tirikadukam
14. Nāladiyār
15. Nāṉmaṇikkadikai
16. Paḻamoḻi Nāṉūṟu
17. Mutumoḻikkāñci
18. Tirukkuṟaḷ

1. **Ācārakkōvai**

The author of this work is known as Peruvāyiṉ Muḷḷiyār. The work lists those modes of behaviour that are considered to be indispensable in life. It consists of one hundred and one poems composed in the metre called *veṇpā*. The fact that this work recommends many indispensable modes of conduct is suggestive that the Tamil land was in a state of social and cultural degradation at the time of the composition of this work.

2. **Iṉṉā Nāṟpatu**

In this work there are forty one verses. Its author is known as Kapilar. This Kapilar is a later Kapilar and not the classical Kapilar we come across in Puṟanāṉūṟu poems. Each of the verses in this piece of work enumerates four bad things which should be eschewed. The verses, in very outspoken terms, condemn alcoholism, gambling, meat-eating and disobedience to one's parents.

3. **Iṉiyavai Nāṟpatu**

The author of this work is Pūtaṉ Centaṉār. In this anthology, there are forty-one verses including the invocatory verse at the beginning. "Iniyavai Nāṟpatu" means forty verses of good advice. But for four verses, all the verses contain three pieces of advice.

4. **Ēlāti**

This is an ethical work. This work was authored by a poet called Kaṇita Mētāviyār. There are eighty two verses in this literary work. It would appear that the author of this work was an astrologer well versed in mathematics. In the Siddha medicine, the word Ēlāti refers to a medical pill the components of which are cardamom, cinnamon, pepper, dried ginger and long pepper. This pill is a panacea for most common illnesses. The implication of the title of this work is that those who observe the commands contained in this work could lead a happy and trouble free life.

5. **Aintiṇai E̲lupatu**

There are seventy verses in this literary work. For each of the five landscapes and motifs there are fourteen verses making a total of seventy verses. A poet called Mūtāviyār is said to be the author of this work. We are able to glean information about the traditions, practices and beliefs of the ancient Tamils from this work. The verses are love poems which vividly depict human feelings.

6. **Kār Nāṟpatu**

In the anthology called the Patiṉeṇkīḻkkaṇakku, out of the eighteen components, twelve components relate to codes of good conduct, six components are on the subject of love and one component is on a subject other than love or good conduct.

Kār Nāṟpatu is one of the six components which are dealing with the subject of love. The verses in this component give a vivid description of the winter season, which is set as the background for depiction of feelings of separation.

After a brief period of courting and dating the boy leaves her girl friend and goes away on the orders of the king to serve in the king's army, which is waging a war within the territory of the enemy. When he bids farewell, he promises to return before the onset of the rainy season. The battle lasted longer than expected. There was delay. The girl waits for the boy hoping that he would come as promised. The blooming of flowers, the humming of bees and the chirping of birds remind her of the arrival of the rainy season. This increases her pangs of separation and she begins to worry for her lover, entertaining various frightening thoughts.

The author of this work was Maturai Kaṇṇaṉ Kūttaṉār.

7. **Kaḷavaḻi Nāṟpatu**

This is the only component in Patiṉeṇkīḻkkaṇakku which speaks of the details of war. The author of this work is Poikaiyār. There are forty one verses in this work.

8. **Aintiṇai Aimpatu**

This is a collection of love poems. In all there are fifty poems. The author of this collection is Māṟaṉ Poṟaiyaṉār. The contents of the poems in this collection reveal the command the author had in the Caṅkam literature. The later commentators on Tamil literature have profusely quoted from this collection.

9. **Kainnilai**

This piece of work contains love poems. Altogether there are sixty verses. For each of the five lands (*Tiṇai*) there are twelve verses, that is twelve verses for *Mullai,* twelve for *Kuṟiñci,* twelve for *Marutam,* twelve for *Neytal* and twelve for *Pālai.* The word *Tiṇai* means not only the land, but also the conduct appropriate to the people of the land according to literary tradition.

"Kai" means conduct in Tamil; "nilai" means nature. So "Kainnilai" means the nature of the conduct. The authorship of this work is ascribed to a poet called Pullaṅkādanār.

10. **Ciṟu Pañca Mūlam**

Ciṟu Pañca Mūlam is the name of a medicinal pill in the *Siddha* system of medicine. The pill is so called because it is prepared from five medicinal herbs such as the root of *Neruñci* (cow thorn), *Solanum xanthocarpum, Solanum indicum, Jasminum angustifolium* and *Arabian jasmine.* The author of this work is Kariyācāṉ. He was a Jain. There are one hundred verses in this work including the prefatory verse. The title suggests that the reading and understanding of each of the 100 verses will teach the reader the path to God and godliness, even as how the pill called Ciṟu Pañca Mūlam will lead to good health.

11. **Tiṇaimālai Nūṟṟaimpatu**

This is a collection of love poems. The author of this work is Kaṇita Mētāviyār. He appears to be the same person who authored the collection called Ēlāti. There are one hundred and fifty verses in this collection with thirty verses for each of the five landscapes and motifs. The literary quality of this work is such that not only the later literary commentators but also Saint Mānickavācakar (author of Tiruvācakam) has employed the expressions and concepts that are contained in it.

12. **Tiṇaimoḻi Aimpatu**

The poems in this collection are also love poems. The authorship of this work is assigned to Kaṇṇaṉ Cēntaṉār. As the title suggests there are fifty poems in this collection. The verses are replete with rhymes, alliterations, similes and metaphors, reminiscent of classical Caṅkam works. There is minimal use of Sanskrit words in this work.

13. **Tirikadukam**

Tirikadukam in Tamil refers to a medicine the components of which are dried ginger, pepper and long pepper. There are one hundred and one poems in this work, set in the Tamil metre called veṇpā. Whereas Tirikadukam is a Siddha medicine for physical illness, the three pieces of advice contained in each of the one hundred and one poems are very good medicine for human beings suffering from incurable mental diseases such as jealousy, avarice, anger and harsh words. The author of the work is Nallātaṉār, a teacher, who is said to have lived during the second century A.D.

14. **Nāladiyār**

This is rated as a highly classical work ranking with the Tirukkuṟaḷ in its eminence. There are four hundred verses excluding the invocatory verse. This is said to be the work of many authors who were Jains by religion. It is said to have been compiled around the 5th century A.D by a poet called Patumaṉār. This was translated into English by Rev.G. U. Pope, the great missionary who introduced the Tamil literary heritage to the Western world.

15. **Nāṉmaṇikkadikai**

There are one hundred and three poems in this collection. Each poem contains four gems of advice strung in a chain of words, hence the title Nāṉmaṇikkadikai. Maṇi means gems; Kadikai means chain. Nāṉ means four. Ancient commentators have spoken highly of this collection. This was authored by a poet called Viḷampi Nākaṉār.

16. **Paḻamoḻi Nāṉūṟu (Four Hundred Proverbs)**

The title of the work means four hundred proverbs. There are four hundred verses in this work and each one contains a proverb in its last line. The poetic metre of these verses is called *veṇpā*, the composition of which type of verse is said to be a challenge even to the most talented poets. The author of the work is Muṉṟuṟai Araiyaṉār. The verses in this work contain important details relating to King Karikālaṉ, King Porkaippāṇdiyaṉ, Pāri, Pēkan and King

Maṉunītikaṇda Cōḻaṉ. These details are of great help in reconstructing the history of ancient Tamils.

17. **Mutumoḻikkāñci**

Mutumoḻi in Tamil means proverb. There are ten chapters in this work each of which contains ten verses making a total of one hundred verses. Each line of the verse contains a pithy proverb. Most of the proverbs dwell on the theme of impermanence. The author of the work is Maturai Kūdalur Kiḻar.

18. **Tirukkuṟaḷ**

Tirukkuṟaḷ is a world classic. In the world of literature there could be few works that could compare with, or surpass it. Tirukkuṟaḷ has all along been such a laudable piece of literature that even Western scholars have made sincere efforts to study it. Rev. G. U. Pope is one among them. The genius of Tiruvaḷḷuvar was so brilliant that his masterpiece influenced Tamil classics such as Puṟanāṉūṟu, Cilappatikāram and Maṇimēkalai. Tirukkuṟaḷ has one thousand three hundred and thirty couplets divided into three main parts; the first part deals with Righteousness or virtue (Aṟattuppāl); the second deals with the importance of learning the art of living, the art of state governmance and the qualities of the nobility and wealth (Porudpāl); and the third deals with Love (Kāmattuppāl). Each chapter contains ten couplets. Free from any sectarian or religious prejudices, Tiruvaḷḷuvar has presented a moral code for the whole humanity, regardless of caste, creed, colour or identity.

Annexe One

Guide to Transliteration

In this work, whenever Tamil or Sanskrit words have been transliterated, including names of people, places and works of literature the system adopted by the Madras University Tamil Lexicon of 1936 has been followed with certain exceptions. Where the Tamil names of plants, flowers etc appear in the transliterated form, in the absence of an English equivalent, italics have been used, e.g. *nerunci, navatpalam, paramparai, panakkarar* etc.

For certain words of Sanskrit origin, however, the readily recognisable forms in ordinary English use have been retained, e.g. Rama, Ravana, Harishchandra, Buddha, Brahma etc rather than their Tamilised equivalents of Raman, Ravanan, Buddhan, Brahman, Ariccantiran etc.

The Tamil consonant "ட்" and the animated consonants in that group present problems in transliteration. Madras Tamil Lexicon prefers the use of t as the closest equivalent of "ட்" on all occasions. I have however in this work deviated from them in certain places. Except in instances where "ட்" is doubled, I have used '**d**' instead of '**ṭ**' e.g. Nāladiyār, Paripādal, Nāṉmaṇikkadikai, Pādal, Tirikadukam, Nedunalvādai, Pādiṉi, Malaipadukadām rather than Nālaṭiyār, Paripāṭal, Nāṉmaṇikkaṭikai, Pāṭal, Tirikaṭukam, Neṭunalvāṭai, Pāṭiṉi, Malaipaṭukaṭām etc.

Annexe Two

LIST OF THE EPISODES CONTAINED IN THIS BOOK

Annexe Three

LIST OF TAMIL WORKS FROM WHICH THE POEMS DEALT WITH IN THIS BOOK HAVE BEEN SELECTED

1. Puṟanāṉūṟu	First Century B.C
2. Kalittokai	First Century A.D
3. Kuṟuntokai	First Century B.C
4. Naṟṟiṇai	First Century B.C
5. Tirukkuṟaḷ	First Century B.C
6. Nāladiyār	Third Century A.D
7. Nāṉmaṇikkadikai	Third Century A.D
8. Aintiṇai Aimpatu	Third Century A.D
9. Tiṇaimālai Nūṟṟaimpatu	Third Century A.D
10. Tēvāram	Seventh Century A.D
11. Tiruvācakam	Ninth Century A.D
12. Kampa rāmāyaṇam	Twelfth Century A.D
13. Works of Avvaiyār	Twelfth Century A.D
14. Ariccantira Purāṇam	Fourteenth Century A.D
15. Vivēka Cintāmaṇi	Sixteenth Century A.D

Annexe Four

BIBLIOGRAPHY

1. Tirukkural – Commentary by Parimelalagar
2. History of Tamil Literature by Dr. M. Varadarajan
3. History of Language by Dr.M.Varadarajan
4. Tamil Verse In Translation by P. N. Appuswami
5. Poems of Love and War by A. K. Ramanujan
6. Ilakkiya Aaraaychchi (Literary Research) by Dr. M. Varadarajan
7. Ilakkiya Marapu (Tamil Literary Tradition) by Dr. M. Varadarajan
8. Kuruntokai (Tamil) Commentary by Dr. U. V. Saminatha Iyer
9. Kuruntokai (Tamil) (Text & Commentary) by T. S. Arangasamy
10. Kalittokai (Text & Commentary) in Tamil by Puliyoor Kesigan
11. Literary Genres in Tamil (English) by A.V. Subramanian
12. The Ankle Bracelet by Alain Danielou

Annexe Five

English translation of The Tamil poems

1. He does not sport the palmyra flower,
nor does he wear the neem.
You sport the Ātti flower,
and so does the one with whom you fight.
Whichever one of you is vanquished,
it is your whole community that suffers.
There cannot be two victors.
So what you are bent upon
will not serve the interests of your people.
If the two of you fight with each other,
that will only encourage your enemies round about.

---

2. Last month this moon shone bright and clear;
then our father was alive
and our hills were not in the hands of foreigners.
This month the same moon shines;
but the plundering kings have seized our hills
and made us orphans.

---

3. Her veins stood out on her shrunken shoulders,
and her stomach looked like a lotus leaf,
she was so old and thin.
News came that on the battlefield
her son could not face the enemy
and turned his back.
Burning with anger, she made a vow:
"If like a coward my son has turned his back,
I shall cut off the breasts that gave him suck!"
Then with sword in hand,she searched the battlefield
drenched in blood.
When she found the body of her son hacked to pieces,
she was happier by far than on the day when he was born.

---

4. "Your years are many, we have heard,
yet not a hair of your head is grey;
what is your secret?"
you ask me wondering.
My noble wife is virtuous
our children are well brought up
my servants give no cause for complaint
my king too protects his citizens;
Above all, my town is full of learned men
with all their passions quenched
humble and modest in all their ways".

---

5. Potter, oh potter!
With him I have come through many a tight spot
like a little white lizard
hugging the spoke of a cart wheel
But now he is gone.
Be kind, I beg you, and make me an urn,
to bury his ashes in this wide earth.
And, you potter, maker of urns for this old town,
make it big enough to hold my ashes too.

---

6. If a child of my family should die,
or if it were born dead,
a mere lump of flesh,
not yet a human being,
they will put it to the sword,
to give it a warrior's death.
So would a king bring a son into this world
and keep him like a dog on a chain?
Or to assuage the fire in his belly,
would he have to beg for a drop of water,
or take his drink like a beggar
from the hands of cruel jailers?

---

7. If only the ripe paddy is cut and rolled into balls,
even the yield of a plot of land less than an acre in size
will be enough to feed an elephant for many days.
But if the elephant were let loose in a field ten times the size,
it would destroy with its feet far more than it could ever eat.
So if a king is wise, and levies taxes that are fair and just,
he will raise millions of pounds,
and his country will enjoy great prosperity.
But if he is weak and thoughtless,
and surrounded by jabbering courtiers
who are nothing but foolish flatterers,
and if he is bent on extorting the most that he can get,
like the elephant let loose in the paddy field,
he will starve and bring his country to ruin.

---

8. Oh my heart, you sorrow for this lad
who once cowered from the stick lifted in mock anger,
when he refused a drink of milk.
Now he is not content with killing elephants with spotted trunks;
this son of the doughty warrior who fell in battle yesterday,
seems unaware of the arrow in his own wound.
With his head of hair plumed like a horse's,
he has fallen on his shield.
Yet his beard is still soft.

---

9. My duty is to bring forth and rear a son,
his father's is to make him noble,
the blacksmith's is to make him a spear,
the king's to set him an example of good conduct.
But to bear a sword, to do battle,
and to slaughter his enemies and their elephants,
that is the duty of this young man.

---

10. Oh land, dear land!
You may have fertile soil,
you may have wilderness,
you may have hollow valleys and high hills.
None of that matters.
Only when the men you raise are good,
can you be called a good land!

---

11. Oh you holy men who walk
under the shadow of your parasols,
to protect you from the burning sun,
with cord-slung pitchers and triple staves
carefully balanced on your shoulders!
Your minds are focused and your senses all controlled;
and you tread this earth out of a sense of duty.
On your way here, did you good men happen to see
my daughter with another woman's son?
They both knew full well what they were doing
and now are joined together as one.

The holy men reply:

We did indeed see them on our way here,
we could not miss them.
So you are the mother of the well dressed girl,
who dared to set out with that handsome boy
along the rough jungle path?
Please listen and reflect.
The fragrant sandal paste is no use to the mountain
from which it comes;
it is only of use to those who apply it to their skin.
When you come to think about it,it is the same with your daughter.
Again the rare, lustrous pearl is no use to the water
in which it was produced,
but only to those who wear it.
When you stop to consider,
it is the same with your daughter.
Similarly, sweet music is no use to the lute
on which it is played,
but only to the player.
When you reflect,
it is the same with your daughter.
There is no point in lamenting the loss of your daughter;
there is no better man that she could have gone off with.
The best course now is for her to stay with him.

---

12. Listen to me, my dark-eyed friend!
Some time ago, a young man used to come by
with a bow and arrows in his hand,
and flowers in his hair.
Supposedly, he had shot and hit his quarry,
and was now in hot pursuit of it.
He would look at me in a way that showed he fancied me,
but he never said a word outright.
My heart was not drawn to him,
but still I could not sleep at night
for the pity that I felt at his distress.
He hesitated to speak his mind,
and I too coyly held my peace.
Some time passed, and then
I did something quite unseemly for a woman.
Just listen to this, my friend with the lovely scent!
One day we went to the farm
where we used to scare off the parrots from the crops.
There I was sitting on the swing
when this young man came past,
still looking at me in the same way as he did before.
I shook off my former modesty, and said,
"Please will you give me a push!"
"Certainly", he said, and I swung to and fro.
Then, pretending to faint, I lost my hold on the rope
and fell backwards into his arms.
He held me firmly,
as I lay content in his embrace.
If I came round too soon,
I was afraid that he would send me home.
So I pretended that I was still unconscious.
He was such a gentleman!

13. Listen to my story, my friend with the glittering bangles.
My mother and I were all alone in the house
when we heard a call from outside:
"Hello there! Please would you give me a drink of water
to quench my thirst"
My mother told me to take him some water in the golden pot.
So when, in all innocence, I took the water to the door,
I was shocked to see who it was that had called.
It was the same troublesome young fellow
who used to follow us around and tease us.
When we built sand castles by the road side he would trample all over them.
He would pull out the flowers we wore in our hair,
and run off with our ball.
When I recognised him, I hid my surprise,
but as I held out the water to him
suddenly he grasped my bangled wrist.
"Mother, look what he is doing!" I cried.
But when my mother came running out
and asked me what the matter was,
I told her,
"The water went down the wrong way as he drank
and he choked on it."
At once my mother patted him gently on the back.
And all the while with a furtive grin
he shot glances at me out of the corner of his eye,
the rascal!

---

14. Just as the eye cannot see the pencil
as it paints the eyebrow,
so when I am close to him,
I cannot see my lover's faults.

---

15. There was no one present to witness
the promise that he made to me on that fateful day.
Only a solitary stork stood still in the shallow water
with thin greenish legs like stalks of millet,
fishing for sprats.
If he breaks his promise and cheats on me,
what on earth can I do?

---

16. What has your mother to do with mine?
Or what relation is my father to yours?
So how did you and I ever get to know each other?
But just as the rain water
takes on the colour of the soil on which it falls,
so when we fell in love,
our hearts became inseparable.

---

17. After kneading the thick yoghurt,
she wiped her hands on her saree.
In her anxiety to finish cooking the meal
before her husband came home,
she had no time to change her clothes.
As she hurriedly prepared the sweet and sour curry,
the steam got in her eyes and made them run.
Unmindful of the discomfort
she called her husband.
But when he sat down to eat
and obviously enjoyed his meal,
her face beamed with pleasure

---

18. It was through my eyes
that this burning love was kindled within me.
Now although it has penetrated
to the marrow of my bones,
still I cannot reach out
and hold him in my arms.
Neither can he come close
to relieve my misery.
Like a pair of cocks fighting on the dung heap,
I am in a fight to the death
with the sickness that assails me.
And there is no one who can rid me of it.

---

19. I am sick at heart, really sick at heart!
At first the cow-thorn with its dainty leaves
puts out fresh flowers;
but later on, its sharp thorns grow
So at first my lover was all kindness,
but he has now turned nasty,
and I am sick at heart.

---

20. A stray pig covered in bristles
approached the farm in search of food.
On a rock by the path
the farmer had set a snare;
but undeterred the pig pressed on.
Then as it neared the rock,
it heard a lizard chirping in a crevice.
Taking that as a warning of some danger,
the intelligent animal at once took fright,
and fled back to its lair.
There are a lot of pigs like that round here!
Although by night my house is closely guarded,
you still dare to come,
waiting for the moment
when the watchman's attention wanders.
What is worse, I cannot sleep
for fear of the risks you run.

---

21. How did this girl become so clever?
When her husband fell on hard times,
she learned to cut her coat according to her cloth,
and refused the treats her father offered her.
As a young child she had been notoriously mischievous.
One day her old nurse brought her
honey and milk in a bright golden pot.
With a cane in her other hand,
the nurse told her to drink her milk.
But she ran off, darting to and fro,
to the tinkling of her pearl-studded anklets.
At last the nurse gave up frustrated by her antics.
How did such a girl become so responsible?

---

22 (a)

"All the resources that men of worth take pains to accumulate should be put to use in doing good to others."

22 (b)

"A proper country is one that runs without besetting famine, constant disease or bitter enemies."

22 (c)

"A region that, in terms of wealth, is self-sufficient deserves to be called a country.

---

23 (a)

Oh king of the mountains,
where the bamboo grows sky high!
Can it be right to forsake your life-long friends
even when they do you wrong?
Will you cut off your finger,
if by accident it pokes you in the eye?

23 (b)

When anger disrupts your friendship
with a worthless fellow,
it is like a crack in the rock.
It can never be put together again.
But when anger disrupts your friendship
with other kinds of people
it is like a crack in a golden bangle.
If you heat it up and beat it,
it can be mended.
But, an arrow shot across the surface of a lake
though will cause a line of ripples for a moment
yet will vanish immediately.
No less quickly fades away
the anger of the upright.

---

24. He that crushes cane to extract the sugar,
sheds no tears when the pulp is burnt to ashes.
So too the wise man labours hard
to fulfil the purpose of his life on earth;
and when the time comes to leave it he will shed no tears.

---

25. There is no member of the body more valued than the eye;
no one is more important to a woman than her husband;
nothing is more precious than your children;
but when it comes to your mother,
not even God comes into the reckoning!

---

26. I have heard them say this often.
Please listen my friend.
When there is only a little water to be had in the forest,
they say that the stag only pretends to drink,
so that the doe may drink her fill
without worrying about him.
That is the path your lover chose to walk.

---

27. I saw a man radiant as the sun;
my wife says she saw a girl radiant as the moon.
Go after them quickly,
and if they are the pair you seek your aim will be achieved.

---

28. He is like fire in dry wood,
like ghee in milk,
like light in an uncut diamond;
in all three, he remains concealed.
If you befriend him truly,
and draw him to you with the cord of love,
he will come and stand before you.

---

29. You pour out the nectar of your grace,
but when I try to drink it down,
because of my past deeds
I choke on it.
Grant to me that I may drink
of that honey-sweet, fresh-flowing stream,
then I shall live indeed.
Master, your servant languishes in deep distress;
You are my only refuge.

---

30. "Make at least one request," said Dasaratha.
The handsome Rama knelt and asked,
"Grant to me that my godly mother Kaikeyi
and Bharatha your son
whom you have disowned
may become my mother and my brother again."
Then all living creatures rose,
lifted up their voice,
and rejoicing sang Rama's praise.

---

31. If only I could get hold of Brahma,
I would wring his necks
until his four remaining heads fell off,
just as Siva did to the fifth one,
for arranging the marriage of this innocent girl
with that old stick of a man!

---

32. "We lost our kingdom,
our son, and all our wealth.
We only hope that there will be
a place for us in heaven.
Even if that too is lost,
never would we dare to tell a lie."
At that, chagrined and speechless,
Vicuvāmittiraṉ vanished.

---

33. The little girl picked what she thought was a blackberry,
but in fact it was a beetle.
So soft was the palm of her hand,
the beetle thought it was a lotus flower.
As it looked around for the nectar.
it chanced to see her moon like face;
then, in fear that the lotus flower would close
when it saw the moon rise,
at once it took wing and flew away.

---

34. It had been raining cats and dogs,
and the floods swept away his house;
the cow was in labour,
his wife was sick equally,
and his servant breathed his last.
Unconcerned, he hurried off to his fields
To sow the seed before the ground dried out.
On his way, the money-lender met him,
demanding to be paid;
the post-man brought notice of another death;
guests came by whom he could not turn away;
the tax man came with a demand for his arrears;
then he was bitten by a snake.
Finally, to cap it all,
the priests turned up with a plea for alms.

---

35. If you think someone is a good man,
and you are very fond of him,
even when he turns out otherwise,
you have to hold your tongue.
For the paddy has its husk,
a flower its faded petals,
and the water its scum.

---

36. One day while playing
a game with poon fruit,
we buried one of them
in the soil at the playground
and totally forgot about it.
Some time later we found it germinate
and we tended the sapling
carefully with milk and butter.
As it grew up luxuriantly
our mother encouraged us
and said that it was like our sister.
What she said stuck in our mind
and we treated it as if it was indeed our sister.
Not knowing this relationship,
you have chosen this spot today
to date with me.
I feel shy to do any courting
near my sister while she watches.
You Lord of the sea shore
that bounds the sea waters
where the spiralled chanks
produce music which is
as sweet as the music of the bards!
Please avoid this spot!
There are many such secret spots around.

---

37. "I sneezed and she blessed me.
And in the same breath
she asked in tears
'Who thought of you now
to prompt your sneeze?"

Annexe Six

List of Tamil poems dealt with in this Book

இரும்பனை வெண்தோடு மலைந்தோன் அல்லன்
கருஞ்சினை வேம்பின் தெரியலோன் அல்லன்
நின்ன கண்ணியும் ஆர்மிடைந்தன்றே நின்னொடு
பொருவோன் கண்ணியும் ஆர்மிடைந்தன்றே
ஒருவீர் தோற்பினும் தோற்பதும் குடியே
இருவீர் வேறல் இயற்கையும் அன்றே, அதனால்
குடிப்பொருள் அன்றுநம் செய்தி, கொடித்தேர்
நும்மோர் அன்ன வேந்தர்க்கு
மெய்ம்மலி உவகை செய்யும் இவ்இகலே!

காட்சி - 1. **புறநானூறு -45**

அற்றைத் திங்கள் அவ்வெண் நிலவில்
எந்தையும் உடையேம் எம் குன்றும் பிறர்கொளார்
இற்றைத் திங்கள் இவ்வெண் நிலவில்
வென்றெறி முரசின் வேந்தர்எம்
குன்றும் கொண்டார் யாம் எந்தையும் இலமே!

காட்சி - 2 **புறநானூறு -112**

நரம்பெழுந் துலறிய நிரம்பா மென்தோள்
முளரி மருங்கின் முதியோள் சிறுவன்
படையழிந்து மாறினன் என்றுபலர் கூற
மண்டு அமர்க்கு உடைந்தனன் ஆயின், உண்டஎன்
முலைஅறுத் திடுவன் யான் எனச் சினைஇக்
கொண்ட வாளொடு படுபிணம் பெயராச்
செங்களம் துழவுவோள் சிதைந்துவே றாகிய
படுமகன் கிடக்கை காணூஉ
ஈன்ற ஞான்றினும் பெரிதுவந் தனளே

காட்சி - 3 **புறநானூறு -278**

யாண்டு பலவாக நரையில வாகுதல்
யாங்கு ஆகியர் என வினவுதிராயின்
மாண்ட என் மனைவியொடு மக்களும் நிரம்பினர்
யான் கண்டனையர் என்இளையரும் வேந்தனும்
அல்லவை செய்யான் காக்கும் அதன்தலை
ஆன்று அவிந்து அடங்கிய கொள்கைச்
சான்றோர் பலர் யான் வாழும் ஊரே!

காட்சி - 4 **புறநானூறு -191**

கலம் செய் கோவே கலம் செய் கோவே!
அச்சுடைச் சாகாட்டு ஆரம் பொருந்திய
சிறு வெண் பல்லி போலத் தன்னொடு
சுரம்பல வந்த எமக்கும் அருளி
வியன் மலர் அகன் பொழில் ஈமத் தாழி
அகலிது வாக வனைமோ
நனந்தலை மூதூர்க் கலம்செய் கோவே!

காட்சி - 5 **புறநானூறு -256**

குழவி இறப்பினும் ஊன்தடி பிறப்பினும்
ஆஅள் அன்று என்று வாளின் தப்பார்
தொடர்ப்படு ஞமலியின் இடர்ப்படுத்து இரீஇய
கேளல் கேளிர் வேளாண் சிறுபதம்
மதுகை இன்றி வயிற்றுத்தீ தணியத்
தாம் இரந்து உண்ணும் அளவை
ஈன்மரோ இவ்வுலகத் தானே!

காட்சி - 6 **புறநானூறு -74**

காய்நெல் அறுத்துக் கவளம் கொளினே
மாநிறைவு இல்லதும் பல்நாட்கு ஆகும்
நூறுசெறு ஆயினும் தமித்துப்புக்கு உணினே
வாய்புகு வதனினும் கால்பெரிது கெடுக்கும்
அறிவுடை வேந்தன் நெறியறிந்து கொளினே
கோடி யாத்து நாடு பெரிது நந்தும்,
மெல்லியன் கிழவன் ஆகி வைகலும்
வரிசை அறியாக் கல்லென் சுற்றமொடு
பரிவுதப எடுக்கும் பிண்டம் நச்சின்
யானை புக்க நிலம் போலத்
தானும் உண்ணான் உலகமும் கெடுமே!

காட்சி - 7 **புறநானூறு - 184**

பால்கொண்டு மடுப்பவும் உண்ணான் ஆகலின்
செறாஅது ஓச்சிய சிறுகோல் அஞ்சி
உயவொடு வருந்தும் மன்னே! இனியே
புகர்நிறம் கொண்ட களிறட்டு ஆனான்
முன்னாள் வீழ்ந்த உரவோர் மகனே!
உன்னிலன் என்னும் புண்ஒன்று அம்பு
மான்உளை அன்ன குடுமித்
தோல் மிசைக் கிடந்த புல்அண லோனே!

காட்சி - 8 **புறநானூறு - 310**

ஈன்று புறந்தருதல் என்தலைக் கடனே
சான்றோன் ஆக்குதல் தந்தைக்குக் கடனே
வேல்வடித்துக் கொடுத்தல் கொல்லற்குக் கடனே
நன்னடை நல்கல் வேந்தர்க்குக் கடனே
ஒளிறுவாள் அருஞ்சமம் முருக்கிக்
களிறு எறிந்து பெயர்தல் காளைக்குக் கடனே

காட்சி - 9 **புறநானூறு -312**

நாடா கொன்றோ காடா கொன்றோ
அவலா கொன்றோ மிசையா கொன்றோ
எவ்வழி நல்லவர் ஆடவர்
அவ்வழி நல்லை வாழிய நிலனே!

காட்சி - 10 **புறநானூறு -187**

எறித்தரு கதிர்தாங்கி ஏந்திய குடைநீழல்
உறித்தாழ்ந்த கரகமும் உரைசான்ற முக்கோலும்
நெறிப்படச் சுவல் அசைஇ வேறுஓரா நெஞ்சத்துக்
குறிப்பு ஏவல் செயல்மாலைக் கொளைநடை அந்தணீர்!
வெவ்விடைச் செலல் மாலை ஒழுக்கத்தீர் இவ்இடை
என்மகள் ஒருத்தியும், பிறள் மகன் ஒருவனும்
தம்முள்ளே புணர்ந்த தாம்அறி புணர்ச்சியர்
அன்னார் இருவரைக் காணிரோ? பெரும!
காணேம் அல்லேம் கண்டனம் கடத்திடை
ஆணெழில் அண்ணலொடு அருஞ்சுரம் முன்னிய
மாண் இழை மடவரல் தாயிர் நீர் போல்திர்!
பலவுறு நாறுஞ்சாந்தம் படுப்பவர்க்கு அல்லதை
மலையுளே பிறப்பினும் மலைக்கு அவைதாம் என்செய்யும்
நினையுங்கால், நும்மகள் நுமக்கும் ஆங்கு அனையளே!
சீர்கெழு வெண்முத்தம் அணிபவர்க்கு அல்லதை
நீருளே பிறப்பினும் நீர்க்கு அவைதாம் என்செய்யும்?
தேருங்கால், நும்மகள் நுமக்கும் ஆங்கு அனையளே!
ஏழ்புணர் இன்னிசை முரல்பவர்க்கு அல்லதை
யாழுளே பிறப்பினும் யாழ்க்கு அவைதாம் என்செய்யும்?
சூழுங்கால் நும்மகள் நுமக்கும் ஆங்கு அனையளே!
எனவாங்கு
இறந்த கற்பினாட்கு எவ்வம் படரன்மின்
சிறந்தானை வழிபடீஇச் சென்றனள்,
அறந்தலை பிரியா ஆறும் மற்று அதுவே!

காட்சி - 11 **கலித்தொகை *(பாலைக்கலி -8)***

கயமலர் உண்கண்ணாய்! காணாய் ஒருவன்
வயமான் அடிதேர்வான் போலத் தொடைமாண்ட
கண்ணியன் வில்லன் வரும் என்னை நோக்குபு,
முன்னத்தில் காட்டுதல் அல்லது, தான்உற்ற
நோய் உரைக்கல்லான், பெயரும்மன், பன்னாளும்
பாயல் பெறேன், படர்கூர்ந்து, அவன்வயின்
சேயேன்மன் யானும் துயர்உழப்பேன், ஆயிடைக்
கண்நின்று கூறுதல் ஆற்றான், அவனாயின்,
பெண்அன்று, உரைத்தல் நமக்காயின், இன்னதூஉம்
காணான் கழிதலும் உண்டு,என்று ஒரு நாள்என்
தோள் நெகிழ்புற்ற துயரால் துணிதந்து, ஓர்
நாண் இன்மை செய்தேன், நறுநுதால்! ஏனல்
இனக்கிளி யாம்கடிந்து ஓம்பும் புனத்து அயல்
ஊசல் ஊர்ந்து ஆட, ஒருஞான்று வந்தானை
ஐய! சிறிது என்னை ஊக்கி, எனக் கூறத்
தையால்! நன்று: என்று அவன் ஊக்கக் கைநெகிழ்பு
பொய்யாக வீழ்ந்தேன் அவன் மார்பில், வாயாச்செத்து
ஒய்யென ஆங்கே எடுத்தனன் கொண்டான் மேல்
மெய்யறியாதேன் போல் கிடந்தேன் மன், ஆயிடை
மெய்யறிந்து ஏற்றெழுவேனாயின், மற்று ஒய்யென
ஒண்குழாய்! செல்க எனக்கூறி விடும்பண்பின்
அங்கண் உடையன் அவன்!

காட்சி - 12 **கலித்தொகை *(குறிஞ்சிக்கலி-1)***

சுடர்த்தொடீஇ! கேளாய் தெருவில் நாம் ஆடும்
மணல் சிற்றில் காலில் சிதையா அடைச்சிய
கோதை பரிந்து வரிப்பந்து கொண்டு ஓடி
நோதக்க செய்யும் சிறுபட்டி, மேலோர்நாள்
அன்னையும் யானும் இருந்தேமா, இல்லீரே!
உண்ணுநீர் வேட்டேன் எனவந்தாற்கு, அன்னை
அடர் பொன் சிரகத்தால் வாக்கிச் சுடர் இழாஅய்!
உண்ணுநீர் ஊட்டி வாஎன்றாள், என யானும்
தன்னை அறியாது சென்றேன், மற்று என்னை
வளை முன்கை பற்றி நலியத் தெருமந்திட்டு
அன்னாய்! இவன் ஒருவன் செய்தது காண் என்றேனா
அன்னை அலறிப் படர்தரத் தன்னையான்
உண்ணுநீர் விக்கினான் என்றேனா, அன்னையும்
தன்னைப் புறம்பழித்து நீவ, மற்று என்னைக்
கடைக்கணால் கொல்வான் போல் நோக்கி, நகைக்கூட்டம்
செய்தான் அக்கள்வன் மகன்

காட்சி - 13 **கலித்தொகை *(குறிஞ்சிக்கலி -15)***

எழுதுங்கால் கோல்காணாக் கண்ணேபோல் கொண்கன்
பழிகாணேன் கண்ட விடத்து

காட்சி - 14 திருக்குறள் 1285

யாரும் இல்லை, தானே கள்வன்
தான் அது பொய்ப்பின் யான் எவன்செய்கோ?
தினைத்தாள் அன்ன சிறுபசுங் காஅல
ஒழுகுநீர் ஆரல் பார்க்கும்
குருகும் உண்டு தான் மணந்த ஞான்றே

காட்சி - 15 குறுந்தொகை -25

யாயும் ஞாயும் யாரா கியரோ
எந்தையும் நுந்தையும் எம்முறைக் கேளிர்?
யானும் நீயும் எவ்வழி அறிதும்
செம்புலப் பெயல்நீர் போல
அன்புடை நெஞ்சம் தாம்கலந் தனவே!

காட்சி - 16 குறுந்தொகை -40

முளிதயிர் பிசைந்த காந்தள் மெல்விரல்
கழுவுறு கலிங்கம் கழாஅது உடீஇக்
குவளை உண்கண் குய்ப்புகை கமழத்
தான் துழந்து அட்ட தீம்புளிப் பாகர்
இனிதெனக் கணவன் உண்டலின்
நுண்ணிதின் மகிழ்ந்தன்று ஒண்ணுதல் முகனே

காட்சி - 17 குறுந்தொகை -167

கண்தர வந்த காம ஒள்ளெரி
என்புற நலியினும் அவரொடு பேணிச்
சென்றுநாம் முயங்கற்கு அருங்காட் சியமே
வந்தஞர் களைதலை அவர் ஆற் றலரே
உய்த்தனர் விடாஅர் பிரித்திடை களையார்
குப்பைக் கோழித் தனிப்போர் போல
விளிவாங்கு விளியின் அல்லது
களைவோர் இலையான் உற்ற நோயே

காட்சி - 18 குறுந்தொகை -305

நோம் என் நெஞ்சே நோம் என் நெஞ்சே
புன்புலத் தமன்ற சிறியிலை நெருஞ்சிக்
கட்கின் புதுமலர் முட்பயந் தாங்கு
இனிய செய்தநம் காதலர்
இன்னா செய்தல் நோம் என் நெஞ்சே!

காட்சி - 19 குறுந்தொகை -202

எய் முள் அன்ன பரூஉமயிர் எருத்தின்
செய்ம்ம் மேவல் சிறுகட் பன்றி
ஓங்குமலை வியன்புலம் படீஇயர் வீங்குபொறி
நூழை நுழையும் பொழுதில் தாழாது
பாங்கர்ப் பக்கத்துப் பல்லி பட்டென
மெல்ல மெல்லப் பிறக்கே பெயர்ந்துதன்
கல்லளைப் பள்ளி வதியும் நாடன்!
எந்தை ஓம்பும் கடியுடை வியன்நகர்த்
துஞ்சாக் காவலர் இகழ்பதம் நோக்கி
இரவின் வரூஉம் அதனினும் கொடிதே
வைகலும் பொருந்தல் ஒல்லாக்
கண்ணொடு வாராஎன் நார்இல் நெஞ்சே!

காட்சி - 20 **நற்றிணை -98**

பிரசம் கலந்த வெண்சுவைத் தீம்பால்
விரிகதிர்ப் பொற்கலத்து ஒருகை ஏந்திப்
புடைப்பின் சுற்றும் பூந்தலைச் சிறுகோல்
உண் என்று ஓக்குபு பிழைப்பத் தெண்ணீர்
முத்தரிப் பொற்சிலம்பு ஒலிப்பத் தத்துற்று
அரிநரைக் கூந்தல் செம்முது செவிலியர்
பரிமெலிந்து ஒழியப் பந்தர் ஓடி
ஏவல் மறுக்கும் சிறுவிளை யாட்டி
அறிவும் ஒழுக்கமும் யாண்டுணர்ந் தனள்கொல்!
கொண்ட கொழுநன் குடிவறன் உற்றெனக்
கொடுத்த தந்தை கொழுஞ்சோறு உள்ளாள்
ஒழுகுநீர் நுணங்கறல் போலப்
பொழுது மறுத்துண்ணும் சிறுமது கையளே!

காட்சி - 21 **நற்றிணை -110**

உறுபசியும் ஓவாப் பிணியும் செறுபகையும்
சேராது இயல்வது நாடு

காட்சி – 22 (a) **திருக்குறள் -734**

நாடென்ப நாடா வளத்தன நாடல்ல
நாட வளந்தரு நாடு

காட்சி – 22 (b) **திருக்குறள் -739**

தாளாற்றித் தந்த பொருளெல்லாம் தக்கார்க்கு
வேளாண்மை செய்தற் பொருட்டு

காட்சி – 22 (c) **திருக்குறள் -212**

கற்பிளவோடு ஒப்பர் கயவர் கடுஞ்சினத்துப்
பொற்பிளவோடு ஒப்பாரும் போல்வாரே-விற்பிடித்து
நீர்கிழிய எய்த வடுப்போல மாறுமே
சீர்ஒழுகு சான்றோர் சினம்

காட்சி-23 **அவ்வையார் பாடல்**

கரும்பாட்டிக் கட்டி சிறுகாலைக் கொண்டார்
துரும்பெழுந்து வேங்கால் துயராண்டு உழவார்
வருந்தி உடம்பின் பயன் கொண்டார் கூற்றம்
வருங்கால் பரிவது இலர்

காட்சி - 24 **நாலடியார் -35**

கண்ணிற் சிறந்த உறுப்பில்லைக் கொண்டானின்
துன்னிய கேளிர் பிறிதில்லை-மக்களின்
ஒண்மைய வாய்ச் சான்ற பொருளில்லை ஈன்றாளோடு
எண்ணக் கடவுளும் இல்

காட்சி - 25 **நான்மணிக்கடிகை -57**

சுனைவாய்ச் சிறுநீரை எய்தாது என்றெண்ணிப்
பிணைமான் இனிதுண்ண வேண்டிக்-கலைமாத்தன்
கள்ளத்தின் ஊச்சும் சுரம் என்பர் காதலர்
உள்ளம் படாந்த நெறி

காட்சி - 26 **ஐந்திணை ஐம்பது -38**

நண்ணிநீர் செல்மின் நமர் அவர் ஆபவேல்
எண்ணிய எண்ணம் எளிதரோ- எண்ணிய
வெஞ்சுடர் அன்னானையான் கண்டேன் கண்டாளாம்
தண்சுடர் அன்னாளைத் தான்

காட்சி - 27 **திணைமாலை நூற்றைம்பது 87**

பிறன் மனை நோக்காத பேராண்மை சான்றோர்க்கு
அறன் ஒன்றோ ஆன்ற ஒழுக்கு

காட்சி - 27 **திருக்குறள் -148**

விறகில் தீயினன் பாலில் படு நெய்போல்
மறைய நின்றுளன் மாமணிச் சோதியான்
உறவுக் கோல் நட்டு உணர்வுக் கயிற்றினால்
முறுக வாங்கிக் கடைய முன்நிற்குமே

காட்சி - 28 **திருநாவுக்கரசர் தேவாரம் -6121**

வழங்கு கின்றாய்க்குன் அருளார் அமுதத்தைவாரிக்கொண்டு
விழுங்குகின்றேன் விக்கினேன் வினையேன் என்விதியின்மையால்
தழங்கரும் தேன்அன்ன தண்ணீர் பருகத் தந்துஉய்யக்கொள்ளாய்
அழுங்குகின்றேன் உடையாய் அடியேன் உன் அடைக்கலமே

காட்சி - 29 **திருவாசகம் அடைக்கலப்பத்து -10**

ஆயினும் உனக்கு அமைந்தது ஒன்றுரை என அழகன்
தீயள் என்று நீ துறந்த என் தெய்வமும் மகனும்
தாயும் தம்பியும் ஆம் வரம் தருக எனத் தாழ்ந்தான்
வாய்திறந்து எழுந்து ஆர்த்தன உயிர் எலாம் வழுத்தி

காட்சி - 30 **கம்பராமாயணம் -4020**

அற்றதலை போக அறாத தலை நான்கினையும்
பற்றித் திருகிப் பறியேனால் -வற்றல்
மரம் அனையானுக்கு இந்த மானை வகுத்திட்ட
பிரமனையான் காணப் பெறின்

காட்சி - 31 **அவ்வையார் தனிப்பாடல்**

பதி இழந்தனம் பாலனை இழந்தனம் படைத்த
நிதி இழந்தனம் இனிநமக்கு உளதென நினைக்கும்
கதி இழக்கினும் கட்டளை இழக்கிலோம் என்றார்
மதி இழந்து தன் வாயிழந்து அருந்தவன் மறைந்தான்

காட்சி - 32 **அரிச்சந்திர புராணம் (மயான காண்டம்) பாடல் -130**

நாவலங் கனியென் றெண்ணி நங்கை தன்கையில் சேர்த்தாள்
மேவிய வண்டு கையைக் கமலம் என்றெண்ணியுந்த
ஆவலோ டவளைக் காண அவள் முகம் மதியென்றெண்ணிப்
பூவினிக் குவியும் என்றே பொள்ளெனப் பறந்ததம்மா

காட்சி - 33 **தனிப்பாடல்**

ஆவீன மழைபொழிய இல்லம் வீழ
அகத்தடியாள் மெய்நோவ அடிமை சாவ
மாவீரம் போகுதென்று விதை கொண்டோட
வழியிலே கடன்காரர் மறித்துக் கொள்ளச்
சாவோலை கொண்டொருவன் எதிரே செல்லத்
தள்ளவொண்ணா விருந்து வரச் சர்ப்பந் தீண்டக்
கோவேந்தர் உழுதுண்ட கடமை கேட்பக்
குருக்கள் வந்து தட்சணைகள் கொடு என்றாரே!

காட்சி - 34 **தனிப்பாடல்**

நல்லார் எனத்தாம் நனிவிரும்பிக் கொண்டாரை
அல்லார் எனினும் அடக்கிக்கொளல் வேண்டும்
நெல்லுக்கு உமியுண்டு நீர்க்கு நுரையு ண்டு
புல்லிதழ் பூவிற்கும் உண்டு

காட்சி - 35 **நாலடியார் -221**

விளையாடு ஆயமொடு வெண்மணல் அழுத்தி
மறந்தனம் துறந்த காழ்முளை அகைய
நெய்பெய் தீம்பால் பெய்து இனிது வளர்த்தது
நும்மினும் சிறந்தது நுவ்வை ஆகும் என்று
அன்னை கூறினாள் புன்னையது நலனே
அம்ம! நாணுதும், நும்மொடு நகையே
விருந்தினர் பாணர் விளர் இசை கடுப்ப
வலம்புரி வான்கோடு நாலும் இலங்குநீர்த்
துறைகெழு கொண்க! நீ நல்கின்
இறைபடு நீழல் பிறவுமார் உளவே!

காட்சி - 36 **நற்றிணை -172**

வழுத்தினாள் தும்மினேன் ஆக அழித்தழுதாள்
யாருள்ளித் தும்மினீர் என்று.

காட்சி - 37 **திருக்குறள் -1317**

Annexe Seven

Transliteration Table

Vowels

அ - a	உ - u	ஐ - ai	ஃ - k̲
ஆ - ā	ஊ - ū	ஒ - o	
இ - i	எ - e	ஓ - ō	
ஈ - ī	ஏ - ē	ஔ - au	

Consonants

க் - k	த் - t	ல் - l
ங் - ṅ	ந் - n	வ் - v
ச் - c	ப் - p	ழ் - l̲
ஞ் - ñ	ம் - m	ள் - ḷ
ட் - ṭ, d	ய் - y	ற் - r̲
ண் - ṇ	ர் - r	ன் - n̲

Annexe Eight

List of unfamiliar names and words in alphabetical order

Ācārakkōvai	ஆசாரக்கோவை
Aiṅkuṟu Nūṟu	ஐங்குறு நூறு
Aintiṇai Aimpatu	ஐந்திணை ஐம்பது
Aintiṇai Eḻupatu	ஐந்திணை எழுபது
Akanāṉūṟu	அகநானூறு
Āḻvārs	ஆழ்வார்
Aṉpiṉ Aintiṇai	அன்பின் ஐந்திணை
Appar	அப்பர்
Ariccantiraṉ	அரிச்சந்திரன்
Aṟivudai Nampi	அறிவுடைநம்பி
Avvaiyār	ஔவையார்
Campantar	சம்பந்தர்
Caṅkam	சங்கம்
Cāttaṉār	சாத்தனார்
Cēkkiḻār	சேக்கிழார்
Cēran Ceṅkuṭṭuvan	சேரன் செங்குட்டுவன்
Cērās	சேரர்
Cilappatikāram	சிலப்பதிகாரம்
Ciṟu Pañca Mūlam	சிறு பஞ்ச மூலம்
Ciṟupāṇaṉ Āṟruppadai	சிறுபாணன் ஆற்றுப்படை
Ciṟṟiṉpam	சிற்றின்பம்
Cīvaka cintāmaṇi	சீவகசிந்தாமணி
Cōḻās	சோழர்
Cuntarar	சுந்தரர்
Ēlāti	ஏலாதி
Eṭṭuttokai	எட்டுத் தொகை

Iḷaṅkō	இளங்கோ
Iṉiyavai Nāṟpatu	இனியவை நாற்பது
Iṉṉā Nāṟpatu	இன்னா நாற்பது
Intiraṉ	இந்திரன்
Iṟaiyaṉār	இறையனார்
Iraṭṭaik kāppiyaṅkaḷ	இரட்டைக்காப்பியங்கள்
Irumpoṟai	இரும்பொறை
Kaikkiḷai	கைக்கிளை
Kainnilai	கைந் நிலை
Kaḷappiras	களப்பிரர்
Kaḷavaḻi Nāṟpatu	களவழி நாற்பது
Kaḷaviyal	களவியல்
Kalittokai	கலித்தொகை
Kampaṉ	கம்பன்
Kampa rāmāyaṇam	கம்பராமாயணம்
Kāñcipuram	காஞ்சிபுரம்
Kār Nāṟpatu	கார் நாற்பது
Karikālaṉ	கரிகாலன்
Karikāl Vaḷavaṉ	கரிகால் வளவன்
Kariyācāṉ	காரியாசான்
Kīrimalai	கீரிமலை
Kōvalaṉ	கோவலன்
Kōvūr Kiḻār	கோவூர்கிழார்
Kuṟiñcippāṭṭu	குறிஞ்சிப்பாட்டு
Kuṟiñcikkali	குறிஞ்சிக்கலி
Kuṟuntokai	குறுந்தொகை
Kūttar Āṟṟuppadai	கூத்தர் ஆற்றுப்படை
Māṉā Maturai	மானா மதுரை
Māṇickavācakar	மாணிக்கவாசகர்

Maṇimēkalai	மணிமேகலை
Maturaikkāñci	மதுரைக்காஞ்சி
Mullaippāṭṭu	முல்லைப்பாட்டு
Mutumoḻikkāñci	முதுமொழிக் காஞ்சி
Nāladiyār	நாலடியார்
Nalam Kiḷḷi	நலங்கிள்ளி
Nāṉmaṇikkadikai	நான்மணிக் கடிகை
Naṟṟiṇai	நற்றிணை
Nāvalpaḻam	நாவல்பழம்
Nāyaṉmārs	நாயன்மார்
Nedum Kiḷḷi	நெடும்கிள்ளி
Nedunalvādai	நெடுநல் வாடை
Neduñceḻiyaṉ	நெடுஞ்செழியன்
Neruñci	நெருஞ்சி
Oṭṭakkūttar	ஒட்டக்கூத்தர்
Pādal	பாடல்
Paḻamoḻi Nāṉūṟu	பழமொழி நானூறு
Paṇakkārar	பணக்காரர்
Pāṇdiyās	பாண்டியர்
Paramparai	பரம்பரை
Pāri	பாரி
Paripādal	பரிபாடல்
Patiṉeṇ kīḻkkaṇakku	பதினெண்கீழ்க்கணக்கு
Patiṟṟuppattu	பதிற்றுப்பத்து
Paṭṭiṉappālai	பட்டினப்பாலை
Patumaṉār	பதுமனார்
Periya Purāṇam	பெரியபுராணம்
Pēriṉpam	பேரின்பம்
Perumpāṇaṉ Āṟṟuppadai	பெரும்பாணன் ஆற்றுப்படை

Peruntiṇai	பெருந்திணை
Picirāntayār	பிசிராந்தையார்
Porunar Āṟṟuppadai	பொருநர் ஆற்றுப்படை
Poruntākkāmam	பொருந்தாக்காமம்
Puṟanāṉūṟu	புறநானூறு
Putuvai Rattiṉaturai	புதுவை இரத்தினதுரை
Taṉippādal	தனிப்பாடல்
Tēvāram	தேவாரம்
Tiṇaimālai Nūṟṟaimpatu	திணைமாலை நூற்றைம்பது
Tiṇaimoḻi Aimpatu	திணைமொழி ஐம்பது
Tirikadukam	திரிகடுகம்
Tirukkētīswaram	திருக்கேதீஸ்வரம்
Tirukkuṟaḷ	திருக்குறள்
Tirukkoṇēswaram	திருக்கோணேஸ்வரம்
Tirumantiram	திருமந்திரம்
Tirumuruka Āṟṟuppadai	திருமுருகாற்றுப்படை
Tirunāvukkaracar	திருநாவுக்கரசர்
Tiruttakka Tēvar	திருத்தக்க தேவர்
Tiruvācakam	திருவாசகம்
Tolkāppiyam	தொல்காப்பியம்
Vaciṭṭaṉ	வசிட்டன்
Vaikai	வைகை
Vēdan	வேடன்
Vettā	வெத்தா
Vicuvāmittiraṉ	விசுவாமித்திரன்
Viḷampi Nākaṉār	விளம்பிநாகனார்
Vivēka Cintāmaṇi	விவேக சிந்தாமணி
Yāḻdēvi	யாழ்தேவி

S. Sriskandarajah was born in Sri Lanka. Having graduated from the University of Madras in India, he became an Advocate of the Supreme Court of Sri Lanka in 1970 and worked in the Ministry of Justice as Crown Counsel and then as a Senior Legal Draftsman until 1980.

Subsequently he moved to Nigeria, where he taught Law and English. Upon coming to England, he obtained a Master's degree in law at the London School of Economics and Political Science (L.S.E), and qualified as a solicitor.

He then joined the Government Legal Service of the UK in which he served as a Principal Legal Officer until his retirement. Currently he is the Principal of CANDS Legal, a Law firm based in Essex, England.

Whereas Mr Sriskandarajah's professional career was in the field of law, Tamil language, literature and arts have been his consuming interest. He is a poet, an experienced radio presenter and public speaker. He is a regular writer, and has contributed many articles both in English and Tamil to various magazines and journals.

While working in Sri Lanka he translated many science text books and legislative enactments. In addition he has written five books, of which two are on the subject of law and the others on matters relating to Tamil ethics and the Tamil liberation struggle.

He is married with two children, one of whom is a legal practitioner and the other a medical doctor.

Mrs Mathini Sriskandarajah is a well known Tamil classical vocalist.